C000180905

BEHIND *the* BAR
GIN

Published in 2022 by Hardie Grant Books,
an imprint of Hardie Grant Publishing

Hardie Grant Books (London)
5th & 6th Floors
52–54 Southwark Street
London SE1 1UN

Hardie Grant Books (Melbourne)
Building 1, 658 Church Street
Richmond, Victoria 3121

hardiegrantbooks.com

British Library Cataloguing-in-Publication Data. A catalogue
record for this book is available from the British Library.

Behind the Bar: Gin
ISBN: 978-1-78488-562-5

10 9 8 7 6 5 4 3 2

Publishing Director: Kajal Mistry
Acting Publishing Director: Emma Hopkin
Editor: Eila Purvis
Design and Art Direction: Maeve Bargman
Illustrations: Ella Ginn
Copy-editor: Vicky Orchard
Proofreader: Kate Wanwimolruk
Indexer: Cathy Heath
Production Controller: Sabeena Atchia

Colour reproduction by p2d
Printed and bound in China by Leo Paper Products Ltd.

BEHIND *the* BAR
GIN

ALIA AKKAM

---

50 Gin Cocktails from
Bars Around the World

Hardie Grant

BOOKS

CONTENTS

INTRODUCTION   6

IN THE MOOD   13

DAY DRINKING   53

UNCONVENTIONAL SERVE   91

AN INTROSPECTIVE EVENING   135

ABOUT THE AUTHOR   172

ACKNOWLEDGEMENTS   173

INDEX   174

INTRODUCTION

One evening in the mid-aughts, during the nascent cocktail renaissance that has yet to cease, I remember sitting at the loungey Pegu Club in New York's Soho neighbourhood sipping a Gin-Gin Mule. The upstairs bar, sadly shut down during the pandemic, was the vision of pioneering bartender Audrey Saunders, and one of the most oft-ordered drinks here was the refreshing gin mule with lime juice, mint and ginger beer. Just as Saunders and Pegu Club significantly moulded present-day bar culture, the Gin-Gin Mule, now regarded as a modern classic, helped reintroduce gin to a flood of new open-minded cocktail enthusiasts. Its approachability even converted vodka fans who were sceptical of this other white spirit reappearing on menus.

Today, gin booms in the US, the UK (the leading exporter of the spirit) and around the world, with some 6,000 different selections on the market. According to the WSTA, in 2021 the UK exported £233 million worth of gin to the EU and £308 million to non-EU countries, while racking up £2.1 billion in total UK sales. Over that same year, the Distilled Spirits Council of the United States reports that nearly 10 million 9-litre cases of gin were sold stateside, generating $1 billion in revenue for distillers.

But to understand this current explosion let's briefly touch on the past. Few eras in American history are as mythologised as that of Prohibition, a stark juxtaposition to the Golden Age of Cocktails that had just flourished. Between 1920 and 1933, when the Volstead Act banned the manufacture, sale and distribution of alcohol, undeterred Americans flouted the oppressive restrictions and found liberation – along with a glorious taste of the forbidden – in clandestine speakeasies. Talented barkeeps, determined to maintain their professional passions, fled to the likes of Cuba and Europe.

Illegal booze, whatever proprietors could find, flowed freely in these underground, largely urban lairs, and it is that seductive image of embracing the verboten that has cemented the Roaring Twenties as glamorous. Yes, there were certainly plenty of flappers descending hidden staircases (one silver lining of Prohibition is that women were now allowed to imbibe alongside men) into jazz-filled rooms, but the reality was far more menacing. Bootlegging incited organised crime and it was not unusual for contaminated industrial alcohol to find its way into these illicit venues, even blinding and killing patrons in the process.

It was an interesting time for gin, though. Whiskey required ageing, yet 'Bathtub Gin' was fast and cheap to make on the sly; all it needed was some water to dilute and juniper to flavour, and its harsh taste could be masked with such bright ingredients as lemon and sugar in mixed drinks. Once Prohibition ended, quality was yet again top of mind, but gin cocktails, a comforting sight to newly re-minted bargoers, didn't wane until the 1950s, mirroring England's own rise and fall of the spirit. That's when vodka – clear, odourless and propped up by savvy advertising and endorsements from the Hollywood set – dovetailed with the post-World War II bounty of shiny appliances and time-saving food products that now lined the kitchen pantry. Gin was a relic burdened by history, and vodka signified the future. In fact, cocktails that normally called for gin, like the Martini, were fast being replaced with vodka. On screen, it's a vodka Martini, shaken, not stirred, of course, that James Bond requests over and over again.

Back in the aughts, when I spent much time at eye-opening bars like the aforementioned Pegu Club, it seemed as if all the new joints opening, not just in the US, but abroad, were re-creations of the speakeasy (at least its more marvellous aspects). These places,

none of which has ever been so finely rendered in my opinion as the late Sasha Petraske's Milk & Honey on New York's Lower East Side, helped spur a classic cocktail revival, and gin played a central role.

Throughout history, a surging interest in cocktails can be traced back to the bartenders who popularised (and sometimes created) them, who impressed their guests with these freshly made drinks firsthand or shared their recipes in wide-reaching books. Some of the libations, admittedly not seen with great frequency on contemporary lists, but that nonetheless helped move the needle on gin, include the Martinez, the Manhattan-esque precursor to the Martini with equal parts gin and sweet vermouth as well as maraschino liqueur and bitters; the Hanky-Panky with sweet vermouth and Fernet Branca from the groundbreaking Ada Coleman, the first woman to lead the Savoy Hotel's American Bar in London; the White Lady, Harry MacElhone's gin riff on the Sidecar with orange liqueur, lemon juice and egg white; and the Casino, which appeared in Harry Craddock's *The Savoy Cocktail Book* as an Aviation variation with crème de violette swapped for orange bitters. In some cases, it's certain gin brands that have made a particular splash. Consider Empress 1908, made at Victoria Distillers in British Columbia. Named for the year the Fairmont Empress Hotel opened in Victoria, the arresting indigo-tinted gin is naturally coloured with a blend of black tea served at the hotel and butterfly pea blossom.

I've already pointed out the importance that Saunders bestowed upon gin early on in the craft cocktail movement (another of her signature drinks, the Earl Grey MarTEAni, reinforces this), but there are many others who were instrumental to the recasting of the spirit, and who continue to champion it through their creations. This is what *Behind the Bar: Gin* magnifies, how bartenders from across the globe are experimenting with gin and letting it stand out in their bar programmes.

Like the first book in this series, *Behind the Bar: 50 Cocktails from the World's Most Iconic Hotels*, my aim is to showcase bars, their cultures and their recipes, but this time through the lens of gin. While there are historic tidbits woven in, there are far more exhaustive resources out there for someone looking to delve into various gin styles, brands, botanicals, production methods and history, and I encourage you to seek them out and expand your knowledge of the spirit.

Some of the featured establishments in this book take pride as gin destinations specifically, but most are bars (and yes, as a nod to my favourite genre, some are in hotels) with a mere soft spot for gin. There are a few recipes in *Behind the Bar: Gin* that are a tad laborious or require ingredients that may involve more planning than a trip to the corner supermarket, but I intentionally included these to appeal to the cocktail adventurists, those who want to elevate their dinner parties with wowing tipples. Most, however, can be made with ease, and all reveal gin's beauty and versatility.

A standard bar kit composed of a shaker, strainer, jigger, barspoon, muddler and ice tongs should do the trick, but you might also want to invest in a cook's blowtorch (it sounds more intimidating than it is) for some of these concoctions that are heightened by a flashy bit of char. All calls for simple syrup are, unless otherwise noted, a 1:1 ratio, so all you need to do is heat a ½ cup of granulated sugar with a ½ cup of water and stir until the sugar is dissolved. Finally, all juices, now that we're long past the cocktail dark ages of the 1970s, 80s and 90s, should always be freshly squeezed to ensure the finest quality.

In some cases, you'll notice that the recipe has been slightly adapted for home use, but I always mention how the bar prepares it so that you are afforded a proper glimpse into their world. Truly, that is my goal with this book, to provide you a snapshot into myriad bars – renowned ones you've long cherished, perhaps, but also new ones that you have never encountered before and are now keen to add to your must-visit list. For so long we were deprived of travel, and I am confident that you will also find *Behind the Bar: Gin* useful as a guidebook.

I've organised the recipes into four different categories that reflect distinct moods, and these are complemented with features spanning such topics as fabled London bartender Salvatore Calabrese and Amsterdam's love for genever cocktails. No matter the time of day, no matter what you're feeling at the moment, it is my hope that I can transport you to a beguiling bar where you will find exactly what you didn't know you were looking for.

THROUGHOUT HISTORY,
A SURGING INTEREST IN
COCKTAILS CAN BE TRACED
BACK TO THE BARTENDERS WHO
POPULARISED (AND SOMETIMES
CREATED) THEM, WHO
IMPRESSED THEIR GUESTS
WITH THESE FRESHLY MADE
DRINKS FIRSTHAND OR
SHARED THEIR RECIPES IN
WIDE-REACHING
BOOKS.

AS SOON AS GUESTS ARRIVE FOR
THE INTIMATE DINNER PARTY,
OR ROLLICKING SOIRÉE AS THE
CASE MAY BE, IT'S ONE OF THESE
REFRESHING TIPPLES YOU WILL
WANT TO GREET THEM WITH.
SOME ARE EFFERVESCENT, SOME
ARE CRISP, SOME REIMAGINE
TRADITION, BUT ALL CONVEY AN
ELEMENT OF WELCOME SURPRISE,
PRIMING THE PALATE FOR ANOTHER
ROUND – AND WHATEVER
SHENANIGANS WILL UNFOLD OVER
THE NEXT FEW HOURS.

ATLAS FRENCH 75

ATLAS, SINGAPORE

Created by Jesse Vida

INGREDIENTS

20 ml (²/₃ fl oz) Champagne
40 ml (1¹/₃ fl oz) dry, citrus-forward gin,
    such as Fords or Citadelle
20 ml (²/₃ fl oz) lemon juice
15 ml (½ fl oz) Simple Syrup (page 9)
10 ml (¹/₃ fl oz) crème de pêche
1 dash of saline solution (combine
    100 ml/3½ fl oz water and 10 g/
    ½ oz salt and mix until dissolved)
lemon twist, to garnish

METHOD

Pour the Champagne into a Champagne flute
and set aside.

Place the gin, lemon juice, simple syrup, crème
de pêche and saline solution in a mixing tin with ice
and shake. Strain into the flute, pouring over the
Champagne.

The bar serves the drink with a candied kumquat
but fresh lemon peel works at home.

Imposing Parkview Square, Singapore's Art Deco-style office tower in Bugis is often dubbed the Batman Building because of its resemblance to Gotham City's fictional architecture. Here, on the ground floor, is the grandiose Atlas. Between murals that wrap the ceiling and motifs that flank doorways, and the melding of bronze and jewel tones, the bar induces awe at every lavish turn. A backlit 8-metre (26-foot)-high gin tower packed with more than 1,300 varieties amassed from locations as wide-ranging as New Zealand, Greece and Virginia, reveals just how giddy Atlas is for the spirit. It also shines in staples like the Martini buoyed by Champagne vinegar and Jesse Vida's riff on the French 75. Named for a World War I cannon, the fizzy aperitif has undergone countless permutations over the years (in the 1920s, Harry MacElhone of Harry's New York Bar in Paris fame dreamed up a recipe with Calvados and grenadine, for one) and is a tad provocative, with a sizable contingent of aficionados believing the drink's origins lie not with gin but Cognac. Vida, who gives his French 75 a boost with peach and salt, is most smitten with its tableside presentation, served 'with a bit of theatrics and spectacle,' as he puts it, befitting of the room.

SAFARI JACKET

BAR TRENCH, TOKYO

Created by Rogerio Igarashi Vaz

INGREDIENTS

20 ml (²⁄₃ fl oz) Monkey 47 gin

20 ml (²⁄₃ fl oz) Lillet Blanc

5 ml (1 teaspoon) Luxardo maraschino

5 ml (1 teaspoon) lemon juice

50 ml (1¾ fl oz) Fever Tree Indian
tonic water

6 dashes of Butterfly absinthe

1 slice of ruby grapefruit, halved, to garnish

METHOD

Pour the gin, Lillet Blanc, maraschino and lemon juice into a rocks glass filled with ice. Stir until chilled. Top up with the tonic. Add the absinthe to the top of the drink. Garnish with the half-slice of grapefruit.

Gin and a powerful hint of absinthe most famously mingle (typically in the company of Lillet Blanc, Cointreau and lemon juice) in the Corpse Reviver No. 2, the bracing morning rouser found in Harry Craddock's legendary 1930 compilation of recipes, *The Savoy Cocktail Book*. At Bar Trench, the combination of gin and absinthe yields the Safari Jacket, a long drink that references the bespoke garment Ernest Hemingway had made by American outfitting company Willis & Geiger back in 1936. Absinthe-passionate co-owner Rogerio Igarashi Vaz is at the helm of the bar, which along with Ebisu neighbours Bar Triad and Bar Tram, comprise Small Axe Inc. He believes that when absinthe is woven into such cocktails in diminutive 'proportions, it can both add some herbal notes and bring out the gin's aromatics'. The Safari Jacket is certainly a suitable libation to revel in during a post-safari sundown, but it's more likely to be enjoyed with equal fervour at the tiny but moody Bar Trench. Awash in black, gold and brick, it has unusually high ceilings for Tokyo, and a glittering bottle display crowned in a petite library that quirkily unites such topics as motorcycles, 1970s poster design and retro Japanese street culture.

SUNDAY GIN

LICORERÍA LIMANTOUR, MEXICO CITY

Created by **Eduardo Nava**

INGREDIENTS

20 ml (²/₃ fl oz) gin
25 ml (¾ fl oz) Tío Pepe sherry
25 ml (¾ fl oz) Vecchio Amaro del Capo
10 ml (¼ fl oz) dry vermouth
50 ml (1¾ fl oz) prosecco
30 ml (1 fl oz) soda water
2 green olives, skewered, to garnish

METHOD

Pour the gin, sherry, amaro, vermouth and prosecco into a highball glass filled with collins or regular ice and top up with soda water. Stir until it's diluted to your taste and garnish with the olive skewer.

Colonia Roma, one of Mexico City's most coveted neighbourhoods, keeps locals and visitors enthralled with its slew of specialty coffee shops, street art-swathed walls and Art Deco mansions. It was a wise decision, then, for Ritual Hospitalidad to open Licorería Limantour in such a vibrant urban setting in 2011. The bar's upbeat vibe and imaginative drinks proved so desirable, that it spawned a second location in posh Polanco two years later. At both, there are favourites like the Margarita al Pastor, a tequila-based reconstruction of the beloved pork-pineapple-coriander tacos that abound in the city, and for the gin fans the Mr Pink with grapefruit, rosemary, basil and hibiscus is a garden-inspired go-to. An alternative, however, is Eduardo Nava's sparkling Sunday Gin. Dominated, in fact, by sherry and amaro, it demonstrates just how nicely the drink's namesake spirit can stand up well to others. For Nava, the creation is a nostalgic one, an ode to carefree alfresco meals relished with family and friends in Orizaba, the Veracruz city he grew up in some four hours away. 'Those days were warm,' he recalls, but whipping up ice-cold highballs like this one always provided much-needed relief from the heat – and 'a good time'.

A HAPPY HOUR INDEED

~~~

THE GIN & TONIC AND THE NEGRONI
WILL NEVER GO OUT OF STYLE

A simple marriage of its namesake components, along with ice and garnish, is all that is required to bring the fresh, quenching Gin & Tonic to life. Of course, the cocktail's permutations – the style of gin, the style of tonic (the rise of premium tonic brands like bartender favourite Fever-Tree changed the game), the additional ingredients – are seemingly infinite, one of the reasons it's popular the world over as a pre-dinner tipple. But it's the Spaniards in particular who sip Gin & Tonics (or gintonic as they call them) from oversized copas de balón with an unparalleled ardour. Whether it's a bar in Seville or San Sebastián, Spain's culinary epicentre where celebrated chefs first gave it the limelight, the drink is ubiquitous.

Sommelier Núria Girós Navarro, who took over the Gin & Tonic destination Elephanta in Barcelona's Gracia neighbourhood in 2008, believes that the cocktail has become emblematic of Spanish bar life not only because of the influx of quality gin brands, but because of its accessibility. Prior to the Gin & Tonic's heyday, Girós Navarro says that simple drinks like vermouth and Rum and Cokes were frequently poured because Spain did not possess a deeply entrenched 'culture of cocktails in other countries like the US or England. Cocktails were perceived as sophisticated products, not for the big audience.

People were "scared" of cocktail bars, snobby places with drinks that people neither knew nor understood.' But there's nothing intimidating about the Gin & Tonic, and it 'allowed a slow and huge transformation', at the bar, she adds, expanding the consumer's palate along the way. Cheerful Elephanta, where some 40 gins, as well as 'Gin of the Month' specials, are organised by classic, fruity, spicy, herbal and citric varieties, reflects Girós Navarro's early mission to 'democratise cocktails' and encourage her customers to transcend the basic vodka and lemon for nuanced, complex creations. Conscious of 'the mental barriers that pulled people back in cocktail choices, I wanted to destroy them,' she says. 'I dreamed of preparing high-quality cocktails in an informal and familiar bar.'

Ordering a daytime-friendly Gin & Tonic is a popular ritual, especially during those carefree hours before a late dinner, much the same way that the Negroni is a staple of the Italian appetite-whetting aperitivo culture. The traditional cocktail, equal parts gin, bitter Campari and sweet vermouth (there has been a countless barrage of variations in recent years) is most often traced back to 1919 Florence. That's when Count Camilo Negroni supposedly requested his usual order of a Campari and sweet vermouth Americano at Café Casoni, except this time around he craved a stronger version. By replacing the Americano's soda water with gin, the Negroni was born. But it's hard to untangle the drink's roots from Milan, the birthplace of Campari, which lends the cocktail its seductive red colour. Milan is also home to Bar Basso, where in 1972 the legendary barman Mirko Stocchetto, who previously worked at Harry's Bar in Venice, accidentally reached for a bottle of sparkling wine instead of gin to make a Negroni. The resulting concoction is the delightful, effervescent accident called the Negroni Sbagliato. These days, Mirko's son Maurizio runs the show at Bar Basso, and the Negroni Sbagliato, served in theatrically voluminous glasses, remains a must-order, sipped against a background that thankfully still oozes retro pink-hued charm.

The Milan bar that exemplifies Negroni culture, though, is Camparino in Galleria, which Davide Campari opened in 1915 as the modern offspring to his father Gaspare's Caffe Campari (Gaspare also created the recipe for Campari in 1860). 'It's one of the gems of the Liberty style,' says head bartender Tommaso Cecca of the bar's movie-set looks, noting mosaic tile painted by Angiolo D'Andrea, a chandelier sculpted by Alessandro Mazzucotelli, a counter made by Eugenio Quarti, and 14-metre-high coffered ceilings, all gorgeous design relics. Camparino in Galleria opens in the morning, an unusually tempting schedule indeed, and all day long it is possible to simply nip in from work or a sightseeing stroll to drink a serendipitous Negroni while standing up, and then quickly resume real life as if the boozy break never occurred. 'This is part of our Italian culture,' adds Cecca. Despite its straightforward three-ingredient build, the Negroni is shockingly easy to mess up, because 'maybe the bartender hasn't used enough ice or hasn't stirred it long enough,' Cecca points out. At Camparino in Galleria, the orange-slice-adorned Negroni is always pristine, and drinking one always evokes the 'prestigious 1920s', as Cecca puts it.

IT'S THE SPANIARDS
IN PARTICULAR WHO SIP
GIN & TONICS (OR GINTONIC
AS THEY CALL THEM) FROM
OVERSIZED COPAS DE BALÓN
WITH AN UNPARALLELED
ARDOUR.

UN TÈ NEL DESERTO
(A TEA IN THE DESERT)

L'ANTIQUARIO, NAPLES

Created by **Alexander Frezza**

INGREDIENTS

60 ml (2 fl oz) gin

60 ml (2 fl oz) brewed mint tea, cold

30 ml (1 fl oz) lime juice

20 ml (²⁄₃ fl oz) muscovado sugar simple
  syrup (page 6)

20 ml (²⁄₃ fl oz) orange curaçao

10 ml (¹⁄₃ fl oz) Fernet

mint sprig, to garnish

Recipe method continues overleaf

Beautiful, chaotic Naples pulsates, seduces, and inevitably tires. After a day of touring Teatro di San Carlo (the world's oldest opera house), strolling by the sea, and devouring la pizza napoletana. sunset means it is time for a seat at L'Antiquario. Peering into the window of this bar in the city's Chiaia area, one notices just how pleased guests look as they spend the evening winding down with a Negroni or Penicillin over the sounds of a live gypsy jazz trio. The atmosphere here is decidedly classy, with a plush ruby-hued banquette, for example, backdropped by botanical-print William Morris wallpaper that has a Japanese-meets-Art Nouveau flourish. Bar staff don spotless white jackets as they painstakingly prepare the classics and originals like Un Tè Nel Deserto, an homage to Moroccan hospitality and the locals who graciously offer just-brewed, fresh mint tea to guests in small glasses seemingly around the clock. 'Transforming this hot drink into a cold cocktail was an interesting exercise for me as a bartender,' admits L'Antiquario owner Alex Frezza. Poured tableside out of a Moroccan silver teapot from on high at L'Antiquario, it's a hypnotic ritual that instantly telegraphs the ancient Medina of Marrakech's meandering alleys.

METHOD

Embrace the 'throwing' method by using two mixing tins. Place the gin, tea, lime juice, simple syrup, curaçao and Fernet in one tin with ice and, with the help of a strainer, pour the cocktail from one tin to the other. After seven to eight passes between the tins, pour the liquid into a teapot filled with several ice cubes. Pour the cocktail from the teapot into a Moroccan mint tea glass and garnish with the mint sprig.

SNAKE-BIT SPROUT

JULEP, HOUSTON

Created by **Alba Huerta**

INGREDIENTS
45 ml (1½ fl oz) Chamomile-Infused Gin*
15 ml (½ fl oz) lime juice
15 ml (½ fl oz) pineapple juice
15 ml (½ fl oz) Simple Syrup (page 9)
45 ml (1½ fl oz) good-quality hard cider
a few dried chamomile buds, to garnish

*For the Chamomile-Infused Gin
(makes 1 litre/34 fl oz)*
1 litre (34 fl oz) London dry gin
30 g (1 oz) dried chamomile, to garnish

METHOD
For the Chamomile-Infused Gin, combine the London dry gin and dried chamomile in a 1.9-litre (2-quart) glass container or other vessel. Cover and let stand for 3 hours. Line a mesh strainer set over a bowl with muslin. Strain the gin through the muslin. Discard the chamomile. Transfer the infused gin to the empty gin bottle or another container with a tight-fitting lid. Store in a cool place for up to a month.

Alba Huerta, born in Mexico and raised in Texas, continually explores Southern drinking culture at Julep, her Houston hangout situated in a former uniform factory dating from the late 19th century. Light and airy, it is kitted out with a copper-topped bar, lace curtains and a back porch for savouring long-forgotten cocktails including the sloe-gin-apricot brandy-lime Charlie Chaplin, invented at the original Waldorf Astoria New York pre-Prohibition. Even more compelling are creations like this quenching reinterpretation of the equal parts stout and cider Snakebite. As Huerta researched resourceful old folk cures in the rural South, she discovered that calming chamomile tinctures came to the rescue of snakebites, plunging her and her team down a rabbit hole that led to a base of gin infused with dried chamomile buds, gorgeously layered with crushed ice and hard cider.

Pour the gin, lime juice, pineapple juice and syrup into a mixing tin with ice. Shake vigorously 20 times. Strain into a collins glass over four 3-cm (1¼-in) ice cubes. Add crushed ice to reach the top of the glass. Top off with the cider. Place a reusable straw in the glass and garnish with a few chamomile buds.

THE FIRST

BAR TRIGONA, KUALA LUMPUR

Created by Emirul Isaac

INGREDIENTS

45 ml (1½ fl oz) Roku
  gin
10 ml (⅓ fl oz) Tío Pepe
  fino sherry
10 ml (⅓ fl oz) lemon
  juice
15 ml (½ fl oz) Basil
  Chilli Syrup*
30 ml (1 fl oz) Herb-
  Infused Kombucha**
lemon twist, to garnish

**For the Basil-Chilli
  Syrup*
½ bird's eye chilli

100 ml (3½ fl oz) water
100 g (3½ oz) caster
  (superfine) sugar
2 basil leaves

***For the Herb-Infused
  Kombucha*
10 g (½ oz) black tea
200 g (7 oz) caster
  (superfine) sugar
1 litre (34 fl oz) water
1 kombucha SCOBY
10 g (½ oz) pegaga
  (Asian pennywort) or
  other leafy green,
  such as sorrel

Recipe method continues overleaf

The Petronas Towers, that duo of geometric skyscrapers designed by the late architect César Pelli, have shaped Kuala Lumpur's skyline since the 1990s. Adjacent to them is the Four Seasons Kuala Lumpur – part of the entertainment and retail hub Kuala Lumpur City Centre – and Bar Trigona is making the Golden Triangle hotel a landmark in its own right. Enveloped in soothing shades of teal and imperial blue and graced by an artful constellation of pendant lights, Bar Trigona is certainly an elegant space to lounge in, but it's propelled by an ambitious cocktail list. Its concoctions are a celebration of truly local ingredients like trigona honey (it's even possible to adopt a Malaysian beehive while sipping a clay pot-aged Last Word), which is incorporated into the bar's signature Old Fashioned with Cynar and cedarwood bitters. Pandan pops up in a churros syrup in one drink and lemongrass falernum and osmanthus orgeat are yoked in another. Whether it's a Gin & Tonic infused with the dried plum known as *asam boi*, sour cherry gin paired with torch ginger flower (*bunga kantan*), or this recipe for a kombucha-capped salute to the native herb pegaga (*gotu kola*), a night at Bar Trigona also promises to be a portal into the soulful Malaysian kitchen.

METHOD

For the Basil-Chilli Syrup, cook the chilli, water and sugar in a frying pan until the sugar has dissolved, then add the basil leaves. Line a mesh strainer set over a sealable container with muslin. Strain the gin through the muslin into the container and store in the refrigerator.

For the Herb-Infused Kombucha, brew the black tea with the sugar and water and once it has reached room temperature, place the mixture in a sealable, sterilised container. Then add the kombucha SCOBY, seal the container and let it sit for a week. After one week, remove the SCOBY, transfer the remaining kombucha to another container and add the pegaga. Let it infuse for about an hour, then use a fine-mesh strain to strain the mixture.

Pour the gin, sherry, lemon juice, syrup and kombucha into a mixing tin. Add ice and shake until diluted. Strain into a coupe and garnish with the lemon twist.

ENVELOPED IN
SOOTHING SHADES OF
TEAL AND IMPERIAL BLUE
AND GRACED BY AN
ARTFUL CONSTELLATION
OF PENDANT LIGHTS,
BAR TRIGONA IS CERTAINLY
AN ELEGANT SPACE
TO LOUNGE IN.

THE HOPE

THE GIN BAR, CAPE TOWN

INGREDIENTS

50 ml (1¾ fl oz) Mediterranean-style gin,
    such as Gin Mare
3 green olives
3 barspoons olive brine
1 handful of fresh basil
200 ml (7 fl oz) Indian tonic water

METHOD

Place the gin, olives, olive brine and a generous
handful of slapped basil (giving the basil a slap
releases all the delicious basil oils) in a Gin & Tonic
or stemless wine glass. Fill the glass with ice, top up
with the tonic and stir.

Back in 2014, The Gin Bar opened as a proper
password-required speakeasy housed in the old
embalming room of a one-time mortuary. Today,
the expanded enterprise (the original boîte is now
home to The Bubbly Bar, which provides a pre-gin
immersion into South Africa's glorious sparkling
Cap Classique wines) is sought after by Cape
Town denizens near and far. Yet the entrance to this
bi-level space drenched in natural light is accessed
solely through the partners' dessert venture,
Honest Chocolate Café, maintaining a whiff of the
mysterious. Over the years, the bar's focus on gin
has yielded a mighty stash of the spirit, with more
than 80 of them made right in South Africa by such
small-batch distilleries as Triple Three Estate, Cape
Saint Blaize and Hout Bay Harbour, and guests taste
their way through them in Martinis and Negronis
while comfortably parked on benches underneath
shimmering vintage chandelier orbs. Another
mainstay of The Gin Bar is a range of quaffable
Gin & Tonics christened 'House Remedies' that
include The Hope, a savoury olive and basil rendition
perfect for knocking back on the courtyard. Covered
in brick, stone, tile and greenery, this lively patch
of the outdoors deftly channels the Mediterranean.

LARKIN G&T

SIDECAR, NEW DELHI

INGREDIENTS

60 ml (2 fl oz) gin

45 ml (1½ fl oz) Roast Pineapple and Honey
 Shrub*

10 ml (⅓ fl oz) lime juice

5 drops of Mace Tincture**

100 ml (3½ fl oz) tonic water

*For the Roast Pineapple and Honey Shrub

12 pineapple quarters

1 kg (2 lb 2 oz) honey

1 litre (34 fl oz) white vinegar

1 litre (34 fl oz) apple cider vinegar

**For the Mace Tincture

15 g (½ oz) mace

100 ml (3½ fl oz) gin

METHOD

For the Roast Pineapple and Honey Shrub, preheat
the oven to 200°C (400°F/gas 6). Roast the
pineapple quarters with the honey and both vinegars
for 30 minutes, turning once. Allow to infuse for
4 days, then strain through a coffee filter or muslin
into a container or sterilised jars. This can be kept
for up to 4 weeks.

Wondrous, dizzying New Delhi requires a
refuge where one can find a spell of peace before
the sensorial onslaught of golden spices and snaking
rickshaw rides resume. The two-storey Sidecar, filled
with books, plants and a bevy of offbeat portraits, is
that place. Founded by Minakshi Singh and Yangdup
Lama, it's where the friendly bartenders make drinks
with local flavours, like first-flush Darjeeling from
the Himalayas, wild borage purée and banana oleo.
A comfy cool-blue chair by the large windows is
just the spot to settle in with a much-loved Larkin
G&T. Bolstered by a roasted pineapple-honey shrub
and mace tincture, it's a salute to the gin-loving
controversial poet, librarian and jazz critic
Philip Larkin.

For the Mace Tincture, add the mace to the gin.
Infuse for 3–4 days. Strain before using. Store in
a dropper brown-glassed dropper. This keeps for
years in a well-sterilised jar.

Add the gin, shrub, lime juice and mace tincture to a
highball glass. Fill the glass with ice, top up with tonic
and stir.

FROM THE SOURCE

SMALL DISTILLERIES ARE CRUCIAL
TO GIN'S BIG MOMENT

London's relationship to gin has evolved greatly over the centuries. In its earliest days it was revered as medicine, an elixir that could come to the rescue of, say, stomach ailments. But the 18th century made way for the Gin Craze, when the cheap spirit, now dubbed Mother's Ruin, unleashed madness and debauchery best captured in William Hogarth's searing 1751 illustration Gin Lane. With more stringent gin-producing rules in place, the spirit found a new audience in the Victorian 1820s, largely at rambunctious gin palaces decked out with chandeliers and mahogany. By the 1950s, UK sales of gin dwindled, as they did in the States, thanks to the perception that the spirit was no longer fashionable, chic vodka nipping at the category's heels.

Bartenders spearheaded gin's recent comeback, but equally important was the advent of craft distilleries. In 2009, Sam Galsworthy, Fairfax Hall and Jared Brown founded Sipsmith. This brand is notable not only because it's one of the most well-wrought modern-day manifestations of London dry gin, but because it allowed craft distilling to return to London. Stymied by the 1823 Gin Act, which made it impossible for distillers to obtain a license for producing less than 1,800 litres (396 gallons), the determined founders courageously appealed the outdated law and won. Now, visitors flock to Sipsmith's West London

distillery, where they can immerse themselves in the gin-making process, just as they do at others that have cropped up in the city since. Another that shouldn't be missed? The Distillery from Portobello Road Gin, a multi-storey destination in Notting Hill that rounds out an up-close look at production with upbeat bars and even guestrooms.

Craft distilling has also shaped the American gin boom. Black-owned Minneapolis distillery Du Nord Social Spirits, founded in 2013 by husband-and-wife Chris and Shanelle Montana, was a hit until it closed to the public, increasing awareness of the brand's products, like Prominence gin. Gin was never a favourite of Chris's, but at the prompting of Shanelle, who loved it, it set him on a new journey. 'I had to learn about my gin, and my learning process was buying all the gin I could find and drinking it in Gin & Tonics, because that's how people were consuming it,' he recalls. One thing that frustrated him was that he mostly tasted tonic. 'The gin wasn't doing the heavy lifting. If we were going to make a gin, we had to know damn well that is our gin in that glass,' he says. Working as an attorney by day and distilling at night, Montana brought in his botanical distillates for fellow lawyers to try until he found the winning recipe, 'an Old World-style gin with a 10:1 ratio of juniper to coriander. By pulling out the different parts the juniper –sweetness, earthiness – we didn't need a bill of 37 botanicals.'

One of the country's biggest craft gin success stories is the New York Distilling Company. Opened in Brooklyn's Williamsburg neighbourhood in 2011, it produces Dorothy Parker and Perry's Tot Navy-Strength gins (that's a term for a robust 114-proof gin that ensured gunpowder would still burn on 18th-century British Navy ships if the liquid accidentally leaked onto it). What also makes New York Distilling Company stand out is The Shanty, the adjacent bar where the spirits made next door are springboards to imaginative cocktails. Here, Allen Katz, founder of both enterprises, weighs in.

WHAT DREW YOU TO GIN?

Gin has always been an integral part of our story and mission. I have lived in New York for 30 years and without exaggeration, the specific fantasy come true was to open an urban distillery here. The thunderbolt moment for me was my first visit to the Plymouth Gin Distillery. There, in the centre of town, was my original inspiration – a beautiful, historic, functional distillery that had been transformed to welcome guests as well. The timeframe also coincided with earnest bartender interest in gin and the increasing availability of a

variety of international styles. Gin provided a blank canvas for us to learn from, to experiment with and, ultimately, to hone our distilling skills with a specific purpose to create original, creative and useful spirits.

HOW DO YOU THINK GIN HAS HELPED SHAPE THE IDENTITY OF THE SHANTY?

We started making rye whiskey and gin the same year we opened. While we put down whiskey without bringing it to market, we really put a lot of effort into promoting Dorothy Parker and Perry's Tot. In our early years, customers would show up to The Shanty expecting to learn every detail about our gins but also to learn about the category more broadly. We have always carried a varied range of gins to help tell the story of our brands with as much relevant history, perspective and flavour as possible.

WHAT ARE THE SHANTY'S BEST-SELLING GIN COCKTAILS?

The 700 Songs Gimlet has been on our menu since we opened. It is a fantastic Gimlet variation featuring Perry's Tot, fresh lime juice, simple syrup, cinnamon bar syrup and Bitterness Hellfire Shrub. We also sell an inordinate amount of Negronis and Martinis.

WHEN THE SHANTY DEBUTED, A DISTILLERY AND BAR HYBRID WAS PIONEERING FOR NEW YORK. WHAT DID YOU PERSONALLY WANT TO BRING TO BROOKLYN WITH THIS UNION?

As a start-up with no marketing budget, The Shanty was our connection to the consuming public and a chance to invite bartenders and retailers during off hours for tours and events to help us share our story and personal perspective on gin and rye whiskey. We envisioned The Shanty as a carefully curated cocktail bar taking as many cues as possible from the 1989 film classic, *Road House*. Sometimes it is a challenge, but we try not to take ourselves too seriously.

ORIGINS

BRITANNIA BAR AT THE BRITANNIA HOTEL, TRONDHEIM

Created by Øyvind Lindgjerdet

INGREDIENTS

20 ml (²/₃ fl oz) Koval Barreled gin

2.5 ml (½ teaspoon) green Chartreuse

20 ml (²/₃ fl oz) apple cordial*

45 ml (1½ fl oz) Ayala Brut Majeur
    Champagne

*For the Apple Cordial (makes 1 litre/34 fl oz)

1 litre (34 fl oz) cloudy apple juice

600 g (1 lb 5 oz) white sugar

10 g (½ oz) malic acid

METHOD

For the Apple Cordial, combine the cloudy apple juice with the white sugar and malic acid. Heat and stir continuously until all of the sugar is dissolved. Let it cool and then store the mixture in the refrigerator for up to 4 weeks.

Pour all the ingredients into a mixing glass with ice and stir. This should remove the bubbles. Strain into a Champagne coupe over a big piece of ice.

Royalty and celebrities have been roosting at Britannia Hotel since its 1870 debut, and the property prides itself on that fabled past. This is apparent at Britannia Bar, an attractive room with arched windows and a silvery, icy palette. Here, Øyvind Lindgjerdet has devoted a section of the menu to spotlighting regional history, with drinks that call to mind Nordic wooden houses or the Napoleonic Gunboat Wars. One of them is the Origins. For this re-creation of the mid-19th-century Champagne Cocktail, that festive fusion of a bitters-soaked sugar cube, ice-cold bubbly and a splash of Cognac that Charles Dickens was reportedly a fan of plying his guests with, Lindgjerdet leaves out the Cognac and bitters. Instead, he swaps in barrel-aged gin and green Chartreuse. To avoid a double punch of acidity from the Champagne and citrus, he also substitutes lemon for good-quality apple juice, mellowed with malic acid (naturally occurring in apples and Champagne) so that it doesn't 'make any noise, blending in well with the complex waves of herbal notes and oak,' he explains. 'I wanted to create something that felt both celebratory and era-appropriate, so I balanced the cocktail around Ayala' – the Britannia Hotel's house Champagne from day one.

POPPY COLLINS

DEAR IRVING, NEW YORK

Created by **Meaghan Dorman**

INGREDIENTS

45 ml (1½ fl oz) Dorothy Parker gin
(the bar also recommends the more
readily available Bombay Dry Gin)
25 ml (¾ fl oz) lemon juice
25 ml (¾ fl oz) Strawberry Syrup*
15 ml (½ fl oz) Giffard rhubarb liqueur
60 ml (2 fl oz) seltzer (approximate)
1 lemon wheel, dusted in strawberry pepper
(the bar grinds dehydrated strawberries
and black pepper in a spice grinder)

*For the Strawberry Syrup
20 strawberries
1.8 kg (4 lb) white sugar

METHOD

Cut the strawberries in half and mix them with the
white sugar in a plastic tub. Seal the tub, label and
leave to soak overnight. The next day, boil 960 ml
(32 fl oz) water. Once it's boiling, remove it from
the heat and add the strawberry-sugar mixture,
making sure the sugar is fully dissolved. Let it sit
for 30 minutes, then strain off the strawberries.

Meaghan Dorman is one of New York's busiest
bartenders, moving to and fro the multiple locations
of Raines Law Room and Dear Irving. At the original
Gramercy Park outpost of the latter, a series of rooms
elicit motley glamorous auras. Likewise, the drinks
by Dorman and her team leave a tasteful imprint.
Take the Poppy Collins, a cheerful transmutation of
the Tom Collins, a boozy lemonade of sorts with gin,
lemon juice, sugar and carbonated water. Credited
with that recipe is the early 19th-century bartender
John Collins, who served it as a punch at the Limmer's
Hotel in London with the Old Tom gin that was in
vogue then. Despite the simplicity of the Tom Collins,
Dorman thinks it remains 'an excellent vehicle for
gin, with the citrus element balancing out the earthy
botanicals and the bubbles carrying the aromatics'.

Allow the syrup to cool to room temperature
before storing the mixture in the refrigerator
for up to a month.

Place the gin, lemon juice, strawberry syrup and
liqueur in a mixing tin with ice and shake. Strain
into an ice-filled collins glass. Top with the seltzer.
Garnish with the strawberry-pepper-dusted
lemon wheel.

MOTHER OF WATER

ALQUÍMICO, CARTAGENA

Created by **Andrey Jaramillo**

INGREDIENTS

30 ml (1 fl oz) gin

75 ml (2½ fl oz) Thyme-and-Lime
  Macerated Pinot Grigio*

15 ml (½ fl oz) Simple Syrup (page 9)

splash of soda water

thyme sprig, to garnish

**For the Thyme-and-Lime-Macerated Pinot
  Grigio (makes 750 ml/25 fl oz)*

750 ml (25 fl oz) Pinot Grigio

50 g (1¾ oz) thyme

2 pared strip of lime zest

METHOD

For the Thyme-and-Lime-Macerated Pinot Grigio,
place the Pinot Grigio, thyme and lime zest in
a sealable container and mix. Cover with a lid
and let sit for 6 hours. Strain.

Place the gin, Pinot Grigio and simple syrup in a
wine or Collins glass and mix. Add ice and top up
with soda water. Garnish with the thyme sprig.

In recent years, Cartagena, on Colombia's
Caribbean coast, has become a magnet for tourists,
beckoning with beaches, some of the world's most
vivid juice blends and a walled Old Town rife with
cobblestone streets and abodes done up in candy-
coloured pastels. Alquímico, Jean Trinh's conversion
of a rambling Colonial mansion into a high-energy
cocktail destination, is also part of this newfound
appeal. Framed by ornate columns, the principal
main-floor bar is surrounded by staircases, curtains
and jars of curious potions, exhibiting an irresistible
air of theatricality. There are bars on the upper level
and rooftop, too, all of them characterised by a trifecta
of menus that offer insight into Colombia's distinctive
culture. This spritzy Mother of Water, for instance,
nods to Colombia's proximity to two oceans and
plentiful rivers and lagoons. Drinks are enlivened
by the likes of corn (married to hibiscus in a syrup,
peach in a shrub), a pine-tree extraction sourced
from Alquímico's own farm in Colombia's coffee belt
that meshes with dehydrated coconut–green tea and
viche, the African-Colombian spirit distilled from raw
sugar cane, fruits and herbs on the country's Pacific
coast. Even classics, the forte of the upstairs bar, are
heightened, say, by the presence of citric golden berry
cordials in Beefeater 24 Gimlets.

AMORA

SCHOFIELD'S BAR, MANCHESTER

Created by Conor Knowles

INGREDIENTS

40ml (1¼ fl oz)
   Infused Gin*
15 ml (½ fl oz) ruby port
10 ml (⅓ fl oz) crème
   de mûre
15 ml (½ fl oz) Simple
   Syrup**
30 ml (1 fl oz) Sour
   Mix***
75 ml (2½ fl oz) soda
   water
1 frozen grape, to
   garnish

*For the Infused Gin
20 g (¾ oz) dried
   blackberry leaf
700 ml (24½ fl oz) gin

**For the Simple Syrup
50 g (1¾ oz) caster
   (superfine) sugar
25 ml (¾ fl oz) water

***For the Sour Mix
50 g (1¾ oz) citric acid
25 ml (¾ fl oz) just-
   boiled, filtered water

Brothers Daniel and Joe Schofield spent ample time behind the sticks of lauded bars before heading back to Manchester. They were reared on the fringes of the northern English city, and so it only felt right to unveil the bar of their dreams (the name Schofield's alludes not to the brothers, but the fire protection company their great-grandfather launched more than a century ago) close to home in the stunning Art Deco Sunlight House dating from the 1930s. Classics are front and centre at Schofield's Bar, and those craving gin will surely be sated by the Clover Club. But there are also such marvels as the Amora, which bartender Conor Knowles likes for its 'flavours and ingredients that I feel are synonymous with wintertime in the UK.' It took Daniel and Joe nearly a decade to conceptualise their first bar together but 'our vision never faltered,' says Joe. 'Dark wood and blues with a design to – hopefully – last a lifetime.'

METHOD

For the Infused Gin, add the dried blackberry leaf to the gin and leave to infuse for 30 minutes. Line a mesh strainer with muslin set over a bowl. Strain the gin through the muslin.

For the Simple Syrup, mix the caster sugar with the hot water. Stir to dissolve.

For the Sour Mix, combine the citric acid with the hot water. Stir to dissolve.

Place the gin, port, crème de mûre, sugar syrup and sour mix in a tall or highball glass and stir. Top with the soda water and garnish with the frozen grape.

THE 1980S' GREATEST HIT

~~~~~~

GOES DOWN AS EASY AS EVER

Unremarkable, often downright abominable, defined the cocktails that emerged in the 1980s. But there was a literal bright spot in the form of the mauve-tinted Bramble. Created in 1984 by the late Dick Bradsell (the bar whizz also invented the Espresso Martini) at Fred's Club in London, this sweet-tart gin sour with lemon juice and simple syrup beckoned with a swirl of blackberry liqueur known as crème de mûre. English bartender Angus Winchester, who as the former global ambassador for Tanqueray played a key role in the rebirth of gin cocktails, is a huge fan of the Singapore-Sling-like drink, 'both as a gin lover and a bartender who worked in an era when for many people gin was disliked,' he says. These folks were turned off by gin, he adds, because they 'traditionally saw it drunk with poor quality tonic or as a Dry Martini that was generally poorly made due to bad vermouth storage and a propensity for bartenders to make it far too dry'. The Bramble, then, was a breezy gateway to exploring the maligned spirit, 'the go-to cocktail for bartenders to use as a way of changing people's minds about gin,' as Winchester puts it. Singling out Bradsell's more obscure libations, including the Wibble (gin, sloe gin, grapefruit juice, lemon juice, simple syrup, crème de mûre) and the gin Cowboy Martini shaken with fresh mint, Winchester notes that although he's seen Bramble variations that star crème de cassis or Chambord, they 'may be tasty but wrong. Traditionally, it was a built cocktail with the crème de mûre laced gently along the top of the crushed-ice-filled glass to give a great visuality, but as fewer bars used crushed ice, some bartenders have learned it as a shaken drink. When asked to settle the argument if it was shaken or built, Dick replied, 'it depends how busy I am', which reinforces why he was such a bartenders' bartender.'

SPONTANEOUSLY PLOPPING DOWN ON A BAR STOOL IN THE MIDDLE OF THE AFTERNOON IS ONE OF LIFE'S MOST FREEING DELIGHTS. THESE BRIGHT LIBATIONS, AT TURNS FLORAL, HERBAL AND FRUIT-FORWARD, SIGNIFY A JOYOUS, FLEETING ESCAPE FROM THE SHACKLES OF OBLIGATION. WHIP UP ONE FOR A LEISURELY BACKYARD BRUNCH OR AS A POST-WORK COMEDOWN BEFORE DINNER.

HAYMAN'S TEA

67 ORANGE STREET, NEW YORK

Created by Karl Franz Williams

INGREDIENTS
60 ml (2 fl oz) Earl-Grey-Infused Gin*
15 ml (½ fl oz) Honey Syrup**
25 ml (¾ fl oz) St-Germain liqueur
25 ml (¾ fl oz) lemon juice
lemon twist, to garnish

*For the Earl-Grey-Infused Gin
5 high-quality Earl Grey teabags
750 ml (25 fl oz) bottle of Hayman's Old
  Tom gin

**For the Honey Syrup
75 g (2½ oz) honey
25 ml (¾ fl oz) hot water

METHOD
For the Earl-Grey-Infused Gin, add the teabags to the gin. Allow it to rest for about 20 minutes or until the colour of the gin is close to that of honey. You can roll the container and/or stir to speed the process. Remove and discard the teabags.

For the Honey Syrup, combine the honey and hot water. Stir until the honey is smooth and flowing.

The heady Harlem Renaissance, an empowering, jazz-fuelled explosion of Black culture and achievement in the 1920s and 30s, forever altered the identity of this Upper Manhattan neighbourhood. 67 Orange Street made its debut in 2008 as the area's pioneering craft-cocktail destination, but its name recalls the downtown address where Almack's Dance Hall, one of the city's first Black-owned bars from Pete Williams, thrived in the 19th century. 67 Orange's owner, Karl Franz Williams (no relation to Pete), helped deepen that narrative of ambition and success. 'Five Points was the first free Black neighbourhood in NYC and as such a precursor to Harlem. Almack's sparked a movement with the creation of tap dance on its floors,' explains Karl. With 67 Orange, he hoped to create a timeless bar that would 'influence socialising in Harlem for years to come'. The exuberant ghosts of the Lenox Lounge and the Savoy Ballroom will always linger in these parts but, for a new generation, 67 Orange Street is just as noteworthy an addition to the Harlem landscape.

Place the gin, honey syrup, St-Germain and lemon juice in a mixing tin with ice and shake. Strain into a coupe or Nick & Nora glass. Garnish with a lemon twist.

I AM GROOT

HERO, NAIROBI

INGREDIENTS

3 chunks of cucumber

4–5 mint leaves

4–5 basil leaves

60 ml (2 fl oz) Hendrick's gin

60 ml (2 fl oz) pineapple juice

25 ml (¾ fl oz) Simple Syrup (page 9)

25 ml (¾ fl oz) lime juice

15 ml (½ fl oz) aquafaba (or 1 egg white)

mint sprig, to garnish

METHOD

Add the cucumber to the base of shaker and muddle. Add the mint and basil leaves and bruise slightly with a muddler. Add the remaining ingredients, strain and pour contents into one side of the shaker then, do a reverse dry shake by removing the ice and shaking again to maximise froth. Double strain into a chilled coupe and garnish with a mint sprig.

Nairobi's cocktail scene is young, but on the upswing. Consider Hero, inside the Trademark Hotel. Food is one of the big draws here, but the heart of Hero is arguably the bar, where ingredients like coconut butter-washed whiskey, cachaça-basil syrup and chocolate-orange-infused tea are frequently reached for. According to Richie Barrow, the hotel's general manager of food and beverage, cocktails in Nairobi were 'traditionally overly sweet and more focused on colour and bizarre garnishes, or incredibly expensive and inaccessible'. By contrast, Hero is meant to be 'a fun and creative space for adults to enjoy and reconnect with their inner child,' he continues, and the bar's everyday libations – including the tropical I Am Groot – reflect that mission. As do the menus. They are accompanied by ever-changing comic books that tackle relevant issues of the day. Moses Obasanjo, aka Lithium – he's known for painting the local matatus, minibuses that double as shared taxis – also covered the walls in radiant street-art murals that bring yet another fantastical dimension to Hero.

FOR THE PAST

~~~~~

SIMON FORD HAS PLAYED
THE LONG GIN GAME

A mid-1990s visit to the Plymouth Gin Distillery in southwest England left a fateful imprint on Simon Ford. 'It was my first time behind the scenes at a distillery. I was hooked. I looked at all the old books and started piecing together the history of gin,' recalls the English spirits luminary. Ford kicked off his career in wine before moving over to the marketing team of Seagram's and eventually working for Plymouth directly, launching the gin in global markets as brand ambassador.

Plymouth, along with powerhouse brands like Tanqueray and Hendrick's, were crucial to rebuilding the gin category, and one vital aspect of this momentum, Ford points out, was the 'up-and-coming bar scene'. In fact, he remembers visiting the late Flatiron Lounge in New York when it was still a construction site and nervously watching owner Julie Reiner turn down a product being hawked by the sales rep in front of him. Ford was frightened she might have the same reaction to Plymouth, but Reiner embraced it, revealing that 'there was this little group of bartenders interested in gin's past,' says Ford.

Distinctly English gins made in the London dry style, such as Beefeater and Tanqueray, were long synonymous with the spirit, but the earthier Plymouth and cucumber-and-rose-infused Hendrick's showcased other enticing possibilities for cocktails. New World gin, a genre that relies heavily on an array of botanicals rather than the trusty juniper that typically dominates the spirit, also contributed to the growth of gin. As the category rapidly widened, Ford was encouraged to launch a gin brand of his own.

That was at the behest of the late, great New York bartender Sasha Petraske, who spent around two years helping Ford hatch a true cocktail gin beloved by bartenders. In collaboration with Charles Maxwell of Thames Distillers, Ford unveiled his London dry Fords Gin in 2012, and now he's followed it up with a not-as-sweet sloe gin in a classy bottle that thoughtfully includes a recipe for his grandmother's version. Sloe gin, coloured a striking red from the sloe berries it's spawned from, is 'the limoncello of England', as Ford describes it, noting how for so long it was made at home, with recipes for it appearing in 19th-century domestic bibles like 'the underrated *Mrs. Beeton's Book of Household Management*. But in the US, it was lumped in with such kitschy drinks as the Harvey Wallbanger.'

Ford's sloe gin is a way to change that mindset while resuscitating a chapter in gin history, one that Ford hopes will see the Sloe Gin Fizz reappear on menus: 'We care about tradition before we break the rules.'

BABA'S SMASH

BABA AU RUM, ATHENS

Created by **Thanos Prunarus**

INGREDIENTS

40 ml (1⅓ fl oz) gin

15 ml (½ fl oz) mastiha

25 ml (¾ fl oz) lemon juice

15 ml (½ fl oz) Simple Syrup (page 9)

5 ml (1 teaspoon) green Chartreuse

2 dashes of Angostura bitters

1 orange slice

7–8 spearmint leaves

1 pared strip of lemon zest, to garnish

METHOD

Place the gin, mastiha, lemon juice, simple syrup, green Chartreuse, bitters, orange slice and spearmint in a mixing tin with ice and shake. Double strain into a chilled coupette. Garnish with the lemon peel.

Rejoicing over good cocktails comes easy in Athens, a city that has bred such hotspots as The Clumsies, The 7 Jokers and Barro Negro. But the bar that kick-started this contemporary evolution is Baba Au Rum, opened by the charismatic veteran bartender Thanos Prunarus (he's also behind the Athens Rum & Whisky Festival and the coffee and boozy pastry shop In Love Again) in 2009. Rum is, of course, the star of the show here, manifesting in drinks like the gingery Spicy Baba and a transcendent Daiquiri. But the boisterous bar is also a democratic one, and so patrons are encouraged to dip into other spirits, too, with maybe the Smokin' Mexican (mezcal, avocado, barbecued paprika) or the Baba's Smash. The sunny Gin Basil Smash is a modern classic first concocted in 2008 by Joerg Meyer, owner of the Hamburg drinking den Le Lion (it originally went by the less catchy Gin Pesto), but the celery-tinted tipple quickly gained traction outside of Germany. Baba's Smash provides a distinctly Greek twist by weaving in mastiha, the spirit seasoned with mastic resin that grows only on trees planted in Chios. Embraced throughout the Mediterranean, mastiha is gaining traction internationally thanks in large part to the educational efforts of premium brand Kleos. Try it in Baba Au Rum's smash, which should be required sipping at any summer fête.

TWO SUNS

OLD GLORY, NASHVILLE

Created by Emily Wilcher

INGREDIENTS
40 ml (1¼ fl oz) Turmeric-Tea-Infused
   Gin*
25 ml (¾ fl oz) orange juice
7.5 ml (¼ fl oz) lemon juice
30 ml (1 fl oz) carrot juice
25 ml (¾ fl oz) Honey Syrup**
dill sprig, to garnish

* For the Turmeric-Tea-Infused Gin
   (makes 1 litre/34 fl oz)
3 turmeric teabags
1 litre (34 fl oz) Fords gin

**For the Honey Syrup
25 g (¾ oz) honey
25 ml (¾ fl oz) warm water

METHOD
For the Turmeric-Tea-Infused Gin, infuse the
turmeric teabags in the gin for 4–5 hours. Remove
the teabags.

For the Honey Syrup, stir the honey and water
together until blended.

White Way Cleaners, a Nashville institution since 1931, abandoned its Edgehill Village headquarters for downtown. But sisters Alexis and Britt Soler, who opened their bar Old Glory in the laundromat's former boiler room, were keen to preserve the soaring smokestack and exposed brick walls, merging them with custom tiles and a storybook staircase to conjure an industrial-chic playground that wouldn't be out of place in their native Miami. Fords Gin is a fixture at the bustling bar, making its way into the Earl Grey G&T and the vegetal Assembly Required with snap peas, yellow Chartreuse, celery bitters and lemon. For the Proper Martini, a clever potable spin on a breakfast favourite, the gin is seasoned with everything bagel spice and melded with cream cheese-washed vermouth. Another hit is the Two Suns. Turmeric-tea-infused gin overlapping with zippy carrot underscores the spirit's enticing versatility. Elsewhere in the city, a few new hospitality projects will soon be graced with the offbeat Soler touch.

Place the gin, orange, lemon and carrot juices and honey syrup in a mixing tin with ice and shake. Strain into a rocks glass over a big ice cube an garnish with the dill sprig.

APPLE-LAUDING

KODA, JAKARTA

Created by **Yutaka Nakashima**

INGREDIENTS

45 ml (1½ fl oz) Bombay Sapphire gin

20 ml (⅔ fl oz) Mancino Bianco Ambrato
vermouth

50 g (1¾ oz) fresh apple, cut into small
chunks

15 ml (½ fl oz) lemon juice

5 g (1 teaspoon) honey

3 small rosemary leaves

pinch of ground cinnamon

apple slice and rosemary leaf, to garnish

METHOD

**Place the gin, vermouth, apple, lemon juice and
honey in a Boston shaker and muddle until the apple
is crushed. Place the rosemary and cinnamon in
the shaker. Add ice and shake. Double strain into
a martini glass. Garnish with the apple slice and
rosemary leaf.**

Koda is concealed in a building in Jakarta's
hectic business district, but those who endeavour
to find it behind one of the six industrial doors lining
a nondescript corridor will soon be rewarded. The
room is a dimly-lit refined one, a luxurious departure
from the snarl of traffic just outside, outfitted with an
abundance of crimson, dark walnut-panelled walls
and a 8-metre (26-foot)-long bar. This is the domain
of Yutaka Nakashima, a dapper Japanese bartender
who garnered a local following at the speakeasy
D.Classic. There is no official menu at Koda, but
Nakashima will happily listen to his customers rattle
off their preferred style, spirit and strength, and
respond accordingly with a drink that magically
matches their mood. If, say, someone requests
something 'refreshing and flavourful' with gin, he
points out, then Nakashima might acquaint them with
his Apple-lauding, in which the aromatic spirit and
just-squeezed apple and lemon fuse with cinnamon,
rosemary and 'the honey and bianco vermouth that
lend it body,' as Nakashima puts it. Given the velvet,
leather and plush carpeting around them, visitors
might also be inclined to stick with the almighty
Martini, perhaps the most gratifying coda of all.

THE SPIRIT OF
A PLACE

~~~~~

BIRMINGHAM REGALES THE GIN LOVERS

Hidden away in a residential area of Birmingham, 40 St Paul's is not a bar that is stumbled upon with regularity. But since its opening at the end of 2015, patrons know that this corner shop-turned-gin hideaway from bartender Amanjot Johal is a place worth venturing to. 'It's a bit far out, in a quiet part of the city, and I felt like it needed a bit of a draw,' recalls Johal, adding that gin was thriving and no other establishment in the city was illuminating the spirit in tandem with the high level of quality he envisioned. It's a formula that worked, because according to Johal, 'people came in, they had great drinks, they had a great time, and they told their friends'. He even takes care of the non-gin drinkers with the likes of Strawberry Daiquiris and vodka-based French Martinis.

40 St Paul's stocks a massive collection of 140 gins, many of which find their way into the bar's much-loved Gin & Tonics, that Johal carefully reassembles with each menu shift. For him, any gin on offer must exhibit 'providence and have a historic context or a good story behind it. It has to taste good and the bottle has to look good,' he explains. 'When you have all of these things together, you want to share those stories. We like giving people information. 40 St Paul's isn't just a place for a drink, it's an educational experience.'

Between flavour maps and questionnaires that try to pare down preferences, it's clear that Johal is keen to engage his guests. Delineating the gins on his backbar to them, imbuing each bottle with a sense of identity through descriptions, for example, of 'a lush green meadow where clover grows is easy to latch onto,' says Johal. 'It transports them to another world.'

ROSE THORN

YVONNE'S, BOSTON

Created by **Bruno Prado**

INGREDIENTS

45 ml (1½ fl oz) Hendrick's gin

25 ml (¾ fl oz) lemon juice

15 ml (½ fl oz) Combier crème de rose
   liqueur

7.5 ml (¼ fl oz) house grenadine

mint sprig, to garnish

METHOD

Place the gin, lemon juice, rose liqueur and
grenadine in a mixing tin and whip-shake –
use just a few pieces of ice and shake until fully
diluted. Pour into a collins glass with crushed ice.
Garnish with the mint sprig.

Boston's esteemed Locke-Ober in Downtown
Crossing was, with roots stretching back 137 years,
one of the oldest American restaurants when it
shuttered in 2012. It was a bastion for the elite, long
a strictly-boys' club where President Kennedy took
meetings and feasted on lobster stew – except for
Mademoiselle Yvonne, Tommaso Juglaris' nude
portrait keeping watch at the entranceway. Locke-
Ober's new iteration, a fashionable supper club
courtesy of COJE Restaurant Group, pays respect
to the restaurant's outsize role in shaping Boston's
early dining scene not only through its name, but
its décor. California artist Charmaine Olivia even
reproduced a modern-day painting of a bare Yvonne.
In the lounge, tin ceiling coffers replicate panels from
the Locke-Ober days, while the library's centrepiece
is the mahogany bar cut from the original carved by
French woodworkers in the late 1800s. Now sporting
Calacatta white marble, it still holds court in the dining
room. During the night, patrons flow through the
different rooms, and postprandial cocktails, several
of them gin-based, are integral to their experience.
These include the Rose Thorn, which intentionally
amplifies Hendrick's floral notes. If a nightcap is on the
horizon, walk a few minutes to the unfussy Silvertone
Bar & Grill. It's been around since 1997, and like
Yvonne's, is a fundamental yet wildly different slice
of Boston bar culture.

DUNES

MAYBE SAMMY, SYDNEY

INGREDIENTS

30 ml (1 fl oz) gin
25 ml (¾ fl oz) fino sherry
30 ml (1 fl oz) watermelon juice
15 ml (½ fl oz) lemon juice
15 ml (½ fl oz) agave syrup
3 dashes of Peychaud's bitters
rosemary sprig, to garnish

METHOD

Place all the ingredients in a mixing tin with ice. Shake. Strain into a coupette. The bar serves the drink crowned with a Flavour Blaster edible rosemary bubble, but a simple rosemary sprig will work just as well.

Prior to the site turning into Bellagio, the resort and casino that invigorated the Strip in 1998 – and generated a revolutionary cocktail programme overseen by 'The Modern Mixologist', Tony Abou-Ganim – it was the Dunes. This kitschy Arabian Nights-themed property with the tagline 'The Miracle in the Desert' bloomed in Vegas in 1955, just as the Strip was being developed into a transporting paradise. That the owners of Maybe Sammy, Vince Lombardo, Stefano Catino, Andrea Gualdi and Martin Hudak, would be taken in by the Dunes' lagoon, V-shaped pool, and vintage Baghdad trappings is not surprising. One glance around their Rat-Pack-influenced Sydney bar in The Rocks and it's obvious the space is a time capsule of its own, a profusion of pink and green, smoked mirrors and wallpaper that channels a bygone Caribbean. That adoration of the Dunes led to an easy-going cocktail of the same name, a Maybe Sammy bestseller that captures the synergy between gin, sherry and watermelon – exactly what one wants before easing into a velvet banquette with a Gibson straight from the Martini trolley or a vintage Negroni with Gordon's and Campari from the hedonistic 1970s.

DRAMA IN THE LBC

THE GIN JOINT, CHARLESTON

Created by **James Bolt**

INGREDIENTS

45 ml (1½ fl oz) barrel-aged gin

30 ml (1 fl oz) lemon juice

75 ml (2½ fl oz) Charred Pineapple Juice*

   (or 75 ml/2½ fl oz pineapple juice mixed

   with 2 teaspoon maple syrup)

30 ml (1 fl oz) Luxardo maraschino

15 ml (½ fl oz) Simple Syrup (page 9)

* For the Charred Pineapple Juice

  (makes 75 ml/2½ fl oz)

1 pineapple

METHOD

For the Charred Pineapple Juice, cut the skin off the pineapple and cut into slices. Grill the pineapple slices in a frying pan until both sides are charred. Once the pineapple slices are properly charred, run them through a juicer.

Place the gin, lemon juice, Charred Pineapple Juice, maraschino and simple syrup in a mixing tin and shake with ice. Strain into a tiki mug or rocks glass. Garnish with mint.

That Jerry Thomas, deemed the father of American mixology, once tended bar at the Mills House (now the Mills House Wyndham Grand Hotel) in Charleston, is ironic. From 1973 to 2005, the state of South Carolina was beleaguered by a bizarre law dictating that all mixed drinks could only be made with liquors poured from bar-cluttering mini bottles. Cocktails, as a result, were astronomically priced and devoid of creativity. The tide turned when The Gin Joint launched in Charleston's compact historic district in 2010. 'When the law was lifted, there was little to no scene for craft cocktails that we were beginning to see in larger cities like New York at the time,' points out Wells Bolt, who took over The Gin Joint with her husband James seven years later. The Gin Joint, adventurous for its time, continues to beguile with concoctions like the Zelda's Flowers (gin, blanc vermouth, apple brandy, lavender bitters, jasmine tea simple syrup) and this tropical-tinged Drama in the LBC (1990s nostalgists will recall that Snoop Dogg kicks off his 1993 hit 'Gin and Juice' with the line 'with so much drama in the L-B-C, it's kind of hard bein' Snoop D-O-double-G'). Few cities embody Southern romance like Charleston, with its barrage of brick and enchanting Rainbow Row. Sitting on the patio at The Gin Joint, in the shade of a loquat tree, is how to quietly soak it up.

ST THOMAS

SPEAK LOW, SHANGHAI

Created by **Shingo Gokan**

INGREDIENTS

30 ml (1 fl oz) Hendrick's gin
60 ml (2 fl oz) Clarified Juice*
7 ml (¼ fl oz) lime juice
7 ml (¼ fl oz) Simple Syrup (page 9)
absinthe (in an atomiser bottle)
dill sprig, to garnish

*For the Clarified Juice
100 ml (3½ fl oz) cucumber juice
100 ml (3½ fl oz) pineapple juice
10 ml (3½ fl oz) lemongrass juice

METHOD

For the Clarified Juice, combine all the juices. Clarify the juice by lining a mesh strainer set over a bowl with muslin and strain the juice through it.

Spritz the absinthe twice into a martini glass. Set aside.

Place the gin, clarified juice mixture, lime juice and simple syrup in a mixing tin with ice. Shake. Strain into the martini glass. Garnish with dill.

Shingo Gokan hails from Japan, and after his golden era in New York working at the magnificent Japanese-style Angel's Share, he returned to Asia. SG Group, his portfolio of Western hospitality concepts, is well-represented in Japan with SG Club, SG Low, Swrl and The Bellwood in Tokyo, as well as El Lequio in Okinawa. He's also helping to raise the profile of shōchū with his own brand of the Japanese distilled beverage. But no recap of Gokan's successes is complete without mentioning his impact on Shanghai. There, Gokan has the bar Sober Company and The Odd Couple, the 1980s-resplendent joint he runs with Steve Schneider of Employees Only fame. Speak Low, the destination that singlehandedly brought cocktails in the city to a new level of imagination is his speakeasy. Accessed through a bookcase in a bar supply shop, guests then ascend to a casual, vivacious bar for a sous-vide Oolong Negroni. Above, there is a slower-paced hideaway for drinks like the St Thomas, a tribute to the track on *Saxophone Colossus*, the pivotal 1956 album from jazz great Sonny Rollins.

THE DEWEY

THE CURATOR COFFEE & COCKTAILS, MANILA

Created by Jericson Co

INGREDIENTS

45 ml (1½ fl oz) dry gin (the bar uses ARC
    Botanical gin, made in the Philippines)
15 ml (½ fl oz) lemon juice
15 ml (½ fl oz) grapefruit juice
15 ml (½ fl oz) Honey Syrup*
2 dashes of Seville orange bitters
lemon wheel, to garnish

*For the Honey Syrup
15 g (½ oz) honey
15 ml (½ fl oz) warm water

METHOD

For the Honey Syrup, stir the honey and water
together until blended.

Place the gin, lemon and grapefruit juices, Honey
Syrup and bitters in a mixing tin with ice. Strain into
a chilled coupe. Garnish with the lemon wheel.

By day, the Curator is a hangout for espresso-powered rendezvous, a place to perk up with weekend coffee slushies on the patio overlooking palm trees, or to snag a bag of roasted-in-Manila beans. When evening comes around, all those orders for single-origin El Salvador brews morph into ones for cocktails, but the Curator never breaks character; it's always chilled-out and friendly. Located in Legazpi Village, in Makati City, an exuberant enclave with a sprawling Sunday farmers' market and restaurants and bars galore, the Curator fits right in, a true community sanctuary where spur-of-the-moment conversations are prized over pretense. One drink that skilfully straddles the territories of daytime splurge and evening rejuvenation is The Dewey, a tangy, gussied-up version of the Greyhound, the highball that simply mixes vodka or gin and grapefruit juice. Customers bask in The Dewey in its unadorned state, how the Curator serves it. But for any home bartenders in search of a garnish, an understated half-rim, say, of vanilla-infused salt (which would turn the cocktail into a kind of Salty Dog), certainly adds verve.

JULIET & ROMEO

THE VIOLET HOUR, CHICAGO

Created by **Toby Maloney**

INGREDIENTS

3 slices of cucumber

3 mint sprigs

tiny pinch of salt

60 ml (2 fl oz) Beefeater gin

25 ml (¾ fl oz) lime juice

25 ml (¾ fl oz) Simple Syrup (page 9)

3 drops of rose water

3 drops of Angostura bitters

1 mint leaf, 1 drop of rose water and 1 drop
    of Angostura bitters, to garnish

METHOD

Muddle the cucumber, mint and pinch of salt in a
mixing tin. Add the gin, lime juice, simple syrup, rose
water and Angostura bitters. Let sit for 30 seconds.
Add ice and shake. Strain into a coupe. Garnish with
a floating mint leaf topped with a drop of rose water,
and a drop of Angostura bitters around the leaf.

The Violet Hour has been around since 2007.
Still, the wonderment that ensues from a visit to the
bar in Chicago's Wicker Park neighbourhood has
not diminished, the curtained partitions, the sea of
cornflower and the layered cocktails every bit as
sexy as they were 15 years ago. Among the enduring
creations is the Juliet & Romeo, a drink, says The
Violet Hour's Toby Maloney, that was made precisely
'for people who loathed gin as much as Mercutio
hates Tybalt'. Or at least thought that they did. It's
hard to fathom that a distaste for the spirit could
provoke a tragedy of Shakespearean proportions,
but there was a time, not so long ago, that die-hard
vodka enthusiasts were adamant that gin would never
pass their lips. Maloney believed his Juliet & Romeo
would change their minds. Similar to the ideal-for-
summer Southside with gin, lime juice, simple syrup
and mint, or New York bartender Sam Ross' Old
Maid that shakes up the Southside formula with the
addition of cucumber, Maloney's drink stands out
for its unanticipated salty notes and complexity. 'The
Angostura is also a cool complement to the gin, and
it juxtaposes the rose and cuke,' he explains. 'It is just
such an easy-drinking drink, but it has a ton of depth
and quirky technique, like the rose water on the
mint leaf.'

TROPICAL SPLENDOUR

GIN'S PLACE IN A WORLD OF RUM

Atop the historic Brooklyn, New York, restaurant Gage & Tollner, a rejuvenated 19th-century destination for Oysters Rockefeller and Baked Alaska, is Sunken Harbor Club, an ode to tropical tipples. Found behind the stick is Garret Richard, who forged a name for himself at New York bars like Prime Meats, The Happiest Hour and Slowly Shirley.

Richard first fell for these whimsical, colourful cocktails in high school, when he worked for a radio station in Los Angeles that played lounge music. Drawn to 1960s instrumental tunes, Richard was then led into the breezy canon of tropical cocktails. By the time he was 20, he had snatched up Jeff 'Beachbum' Berry's masterful books on the subject, and it was while reading one of these that Richard first encountered the tropical Saturn cocktail. Berry wrote of finding a commemorative glass emblazoned with J 'Popo' Galsini's award-winning recipe for the drink (gin, velvet falernum, lemon juice, orgeat) in an antiques shop and then never coming across it again.

The Saturn is significant to Richard for several reasons. First, it was created in 1967, a time that is most often described as bleak for cocktails. But the drink shows that there actually were interesting recipes being developed, too, especially among the Filipino bartenders in Los Angeles who were proactive on the cocktail competition circuit. Some drinks from this era, says Richard, were 'driven by new products like Midori and Galliano, but the Saturn is pretty classic for the late 60s. It could have been made decades earlier.'

A petite crushed ice drink served at the beginning of the meal, 'the Saturn was more delicate and refined,' points out Richard. Although Sunken Harbor Club represents a diversity of spirits and styles of drinks on its menu, most tropical cocktails are historically made with rum, 'dependent upon syrup and integrity of ingredients and the knowledge of how to prepare them,' explains Richard, 'so there's quite a gap when drinks like the Saturn try to cross over.' The Saturn may never be as well-known as a Mai Tai or Zombie, but according to Richard, 'it's a good option when a menu leans rum-heavy'.

He cites the Tiki-Ti in Los Angeles as an example of the Saturn's relevance. Up until recently, the bar, which first opened in 1961, amassed over 90 drinks on its menu, but nonetheless added in the Saturn to sate budding gin drinkers. That menu has now been whittled down, but the Saturn remains. It's a cocktail, adds Richard, that serves 'as an interesting window into what could have been' a vastly altered tropical movement.

BEES TEASE

DRUID BAR, BELGRADE

INGREDIENTS

60 ml (2 fl oz) gin
30 ml (1 fl oz) lemon juice
20 ml (²/₃ fl oz) Honey Syrup*
10 ml (¹/₃ fl oz) green Chartreuse
rosemary sprig, to garnish

*For the Honey Syrup
120 g (4 oz) honey
120 ml (4 oz) warm water

METHOD

For the Honey Syrup, stir the honey and water together until blended.

Place the gin, lemon juice, Honey Syrup and green Chartreuse in a mixing tin with ice and shake. Strain into a Nick & Nora glass. Garnish with the fresh rosemary.

Close to Kalemegdan, Belgrade's most famous park poised at the intersection of the Sava and Danube Rivers, is Druid Bar. An inviting green light above the black door is the only sign of life at this side-street lair, but once they ring the bell and make it inside, patrons feel as if they've serendipitously happened upon a convivial, old-fashioned salon, with a whirling record player and drinks served on quaint doilies. Behind the undulating bar, which takes centre stage against walls painted the colour of basil, silk-vested bartenders prepare the classics – and their elevated takes on them – with precision. There is no official menu at Druid Bar, but along with the regular calls for Martinis and Negronis, those in the know spring for a Bees Tease, an herbal reinterpretation of the gin-lemon-honey Bee's Knees, reportedly invented in 1929 by socialite and Titanic survivor 'the unsinkable Molly Brown'. It's difficult to part company with the comforting environs reminiscent of Grandma's living room, but only a few minutes away from Druid Bar are Bar Central and Belgrade Cocktail Club. Recognised for having set the city's impressive cocktail scene in motion, they are both worthy stops for another few rounds – and insight into an evolving Belgrade.

SHINKO SOUR

SHINKO, CAIRO

Created by **Walid Merhi**

INGREDIENTS
60 ml (2 fl oz) Thyme-Infused Gin*
30 ml (1 fl oz) verjus
30 ml (1 fl oz) orange flower honey
thyme sprig and olive oil, to garnish

For the Thyme-Infused Gin
1 litre (34 fl oz) gin
2 limes
20 g (¾ oz) thyme sprigs

METHOD
For the Infused Gin, pour the gin into a Mason jar. Wash the limes, cut them into eight pieces and add to the gin. Wash the thyme (the bar uses the wild variety), dry it, then add to the jar. Both the lime and thyme should be submerged at all times. Keep the jar sealed in a dry and dark place. Shake the jar lightly every 12 hours for 5 days. Double strain the gin through a coffee filter or muslin-lined sieve into a sterilised bottle and seal.

Place the gin, verjus and honey in a mixing tin with ice and shake vigorously. Double strain into a rocks

Egypt, a country dominated by Islam, is not synonymous with drinking culture. Yet in progressive Cairo, it is possible for foreigners and non-Muslims (and those who choose to abide by a looser set of religious rules) to relax with an Egyptian Stella beer or even a quality mixed drink. Baky Hospitality has a number of restaurants in the city, including the powerhouse group's Shinko, a lounge with Japanese flair and a DJ where guests embark on one of two innovative cocktail routes. They can come already armed with their favourite bottle of liquor, which the bartenders will then adroitly parlay into creative cocktails on the fly. Or they can choose from Shinko's own exploratory menu of drinks, which revolve around Egyptian spirits that are redistilled with local fruits, vegetables and spices in a rotary evaporator, offering a liquid dive into the country's culinary culture. Compounded by the crystal chandelier, emerald curtains and dark marble walls, the watermelon brine Martini, and bee pollen gin fizz all build up to a beverage experience unlike any other in Cairo.

glass over new ice, preferably a large single chunk. Garnish with the thyme sprig and a few drops of olive oil on top.

MY LADY GARDEN

THREE SHEETS, LONDON

Created by Noel and Max Venning

INGREDIENTS

45 ml (1½ fl oz) Porter's Tropical Old Tom
   gin (Bombay Sapphire is a more readily
   available alternative)
5 ml (1 teaspoon) raspberry liqueur (the bar
   uses Louis Roque)
15 ml (½ fl oz) Honey-Orange Flower
   Syrup*
20ml (²/₃ fl oz) freshly squeezed lemon
   juice
15 ml (½ fl oz) egg white
1 pared strip of lemon zest, to garnish

*For the Honey-Orange Flower Syrup
100 ml (3½ fl oz) acacia honey
300 ml (10 fl oz) rich Simple Syrup
   (a 2:1 ratio, see page 9)
2.5 ml (½ teaspoon) orange flower water

Recipe method continues overleaf

At the turn of the 20th century, Florodora was an Edwardian musical comedy on Broadway, by way of London, in which 'Florodora Girls' donning pink costumes paraded across the stage. This theatrical routine begat the Floradora, a light-hearted cocktail with a tweaked spelling that exemplified the harmonious relationship between raspberry and gin (and a jolt of ginger ale). Deservedly overshadowing the Floradora, however, is the frothy magenta-toned Clover Club. Before it was a cocktail, it was what a late 19th-century group of elite males who regularly convened at the former Bellevue-Stratford Hotel in Philadelphia called their animated gatherings. While the dainty drink did eventually lose out to stiffer libations, Noel Venning, who runs the London bar Three Sheets with his brother Max in the Dalston neighbourhood, is on board with the Clover Club's comeback. 'It's a great classic that has stood the test of time both in its original form and with its ability to be adapted and updated – like we have done – as time has passed,' says Noel. The Brothers Venning are forever reimagining cocktails (the carbonated French 75 with Moscato and orange flower is an essential introduction to the menu) and their Clover Club experiments culminated in My Lady Garden, a collaboration with the namesake Dalston florist that plays with notes of honey and orange water.

Typically, the bar makes this drink by infusing the gin
with makrut lime, mixing it with petitgrain honey, and
garnishing it with a vodka-lemon zest spray. This is
the bar's more home-friendly alternative.

METHOD

For the Honey-Orange Flower Syrup, combine
the honey with the rich sugar syrup and orange
flower water in a jug and stir vigorously. Store the
mixture in a sterilised bottle; it will keep indefinitely.

Place the gin, raspberry liqueur, syrup, lemon juice
and egg white in a mixing tin and dry shake without
ice to emulsify ingredients. Add ice and shake hard
for 30 seconds until properly chilled and diluted.
Double strain into a Nick & Nora glass, then twist the
lemon zest, peel side down, over the glass to express
citrus oil on to the drink's surface and garnish with
the expressed lemon zest.

SOME COCKTAILS
ARE CRAVED FOR THEIR
SIMPLICITY, FOR THE NIGHT-TIME
REASSURANCE THAT AMELIORATES
A TOPSY-TURVY DAY. OTHERS,
LIKE THESE, ARE CHOSEN FOR
THEIR SUBTLE OR BRAZEN
NOVELTY – FOR THEIR CAPACITY
TO INTRIGUE, TO RE-EVALUATE
TRADITIONAL INGREDIENT USES,
TO GIVE PEP TO THE
ORDINARY.

UNCONVENTIAL
SERVE

GRANDE GIMLET

TJOGET, STOCKHOLM

Created by **Leo Lahti**

INGREDIENTS

40 ml (1¼ fl oz) gin
10 ml (⅓ fl oz) Coconut Chartreuse*
10 ml (⅓ fl oz) manzanilla sherry
40 ml (1¼ fl oz) Lime-Grapefruit Cordial**
2 dashes of Coconut Blast***

*For the Coconut Chartreuse
10 g (½ oz) coconut oil
70 ml (2½ fl oz) green Chartreuse

**For the Lime-Grapefruit Cordial
5 large limes
1 red grapefruit
100 g (3½ oz) sugar

***For the Coconut Blast
50 g (1¾ oz) coconut oil
100 ml (3½ fl oz) vodka

Recipe method continues overleaf

Hornstull is on the western end of Stockholm's Södermalm island, a former working-class neighbourhood that has given way to a flood of restaurants, bars and shops that resonate with a new breed of creatives. Instrumental to Hornstull's rising cachet over the years is Tjoget, the multi-enterprise complex that Andreas Bergman and Joel Söderbäck opened in 2012. Encompassing a dining room, wine bodega, beer café and zinc-clad wood bar for cocktailing, Tjoget takes cues from Southern Europe, the Middle East and North Africa. There are Mint Juleps, for instance, with saffron, cardamom and rose water, and mezcal-Port drinks that are vivified with sun-dried tomato syrup. Aquavit, sherry and the navy-strength Fords Gin Officers' Reserve are interlaced in the Merchant Martini, but it's the entanglement of gin, green Chartreuse and coconut in his uplifting Grande Gimlet that Tjoget's Leo Lahti is most stirred by. 'It's such a great combination that really opens up the Chartreuse for a much wider use than just classic-style herbal cocktails,' Lahti says of his ingenious variation on the basic gin-and-lime Gimlet, 'and brings it into the world of tropical and fun drinks, something that we really need more of here in Sweden.'

METHOD

For the Coconut Chartreuse, melt the coconut oil and add to a container with the green Chartreuse. Let sit at room temperature for 2 hours, stirring several times an hour. After 2 hours, put the mixture in the freezer for at least 12 hours.

Take it out, lift off the layer of frozen fat and filter through a coffee filter into another container. Repeat if necessary.

For the Lime-Grapefruit Cordial, peel the limes and grapefruit and reserve. Juice the fruits and measure out 80 ml (2½ fl oz) of lime juice and 20 ml (⅔ fl oz) of grapefruit. Juice more fruit if needed, but there's no need to peel those. Combine the juices and add the sugar. Stir until the sugar is dissolved and add the peels. Cover and put in the refrigerator for 24 hours, then strain.

For the Coconut Blast, melt the coconut oil and add to a container with the vodka. Let sit at room temperature for 2 hours, stirring several times an hour. After 2 hours, put it in the freezer and let it sit for at least 12 hours. Take it out, lift off the frozen fat and filter through a coffee filter. Repeat if necessary.

Place the gin, coconut Chartreuse, sherry, cordial and Coconut Blast in a mixing tin with ice and shake. Strain into a coupette.

ENCOMPASSING
A DINING ROOM,
WINE BODEGA, BEER CAFÉ
AND ZINC-CLAD WOOD BAR
FOR COCKTAILING,
TJOGET TAKES CUES
FROM SOUTHERN EUROPE,
THE MIDDLE EAST
AND NORTH AFRICA.

NASHI & MATCHA

ORIGIN AT SHANGRI-LA SINGAPORE

Created by **Adam Bursik**

INGREDIENTS

45 ml (1½ fl oz) Roku gin
25 ml (¾ fl oz) Nashi Cordial*
90 ml (3 fl oz) London Essence tonic water
20 ml (⅔ fl oz) Matcha Tea Float**
slice of Nashi (or other variety) pear,
   to garnish

*For the Nashi Cordial

1.2 kg (2 lb 11 oz) caster (superfine) sugar
2 litres (70 fl oz) pear juice (ideally Nashi)
60 g (2 oz) ascorbic acid

**For the Matcha Tea Float

2 teaspoons matcha tea
200 ml (7 fl oz) water

Recipe method continues overleaf

Defined by its verdant tropical gardens, the upscale Shangri-La Singapore has been one of the island's most clamoured-for hotels since opening in 1971. Of the more modern interventions at this grande dame is Origin Grill & Bar, a sequence of arched rooms modelled on the train stations of yesteryear. Before moving onto dinner, guests sit in the drenched-in-blue Origin Bar and order cocktails with pickled ginger, nutmeg, yuzu, lemongrass and fermented pepper off a menu that serves as a miniature history lesson on the island. Organised into six of Singapore's most important districts – Orchard, Balestier, Chinatown, Little India, Boat Quay and Marina Bay – the list magnifies Singapore's days as a prosperous British trading post in the 19th century and confirms that its status as a stimulating melting pot remains intact. The Nashi & Matcha, a sophisticated pear and green tea highball, resides in the menu's Boat Quay section, which, explains Origin Bar's Adam Bursik, refers to the old Port of Singapore and the part of it that drummed up the most shipping business. Boat Quay, Bursik adds, 'represents new cultures and new ingredients coming to Singapore. We used the Nashi & Matcha to bring in flavours that are common in Japan.'

METHOD

For the Nashi Cordial, melt 600 g (1 lb 5 oz) of the sugar to the point of caramelisation, then add the pear juice (the bar uses the especially juicy Nashi but any variety will work) and let it dissolve. Add the remaining sugar and ascorbic acid (this will lend acidity to the drink; if it's not readily available, then mix 10 ml ($^1/_3$ fl oz) lemon juice with the gin and cordial) and let the mixture slowly simmer for a good 25 minutes.

Pour the gin, cordial and tonic into a highball glass. Place an ice spear in the glass and mix with a barspoon, gently lifting and lowering the ice spear.

For the Matcha Tea Float, add the matcha tea to the water. Place in a small squeeze bottle and shake well until all the tea is dissolved and frothy. Then, using a spoon, float it atop the cocktail to create a new layer. Garnish with the pear slice.

OF THE MORE
MODERN INTERVENTIONS
AT THIS GRANDE DAME IS
ORIGIN GRILL & BAR,
A SEQUENCE OF ARCHED
ROOMS MODELLED ON
THE TRAIN STATIONS
OF YESTERYEAR.

BLACK VELVET

THE DRESDEN RESTAURANT & LOUNGE, LOS ANGELES

Created by **Mark Ferraro**

INGREDIENTS

60 ml (2 fl oz) Nolet's dry gin

15 ml (½ fl oz) Luxardo Bitter Bianco

7.5 ml (¼ fl oz) blackberry syrup

9 dashes of Fee Brothers lavender water
    (the bar uses nine, but feel free to adjust
    down based on preferred strength)

expressed lemon peel skewered with
    a blackberry, to garnish

METHOD

Place the gin, Luxardo, blackberry syrup and lavender water in a mixing glass with ice and stir. Strain into a Nick & Nora glass and garnish with skewer of expressed lemon peel and a blackberry.

Vista Theatre, the single-screen cinema with the showy Spanish-Colonial Revival façade and splendorous Egyptian interiors, has been a Los Feliz attraction since 1923, an audacious architectural symbol of the hilly neighbourhood's proximity to Hollywood's flash. It's mere minutes from there to the Dresden Restaurant & Lounge, where little has changed since its 1955 unveiling. The Dresden made a cameo in the 1996 comedy-drama *Swingers*, in the memorable 'you're so money' scene. But old-timers knew long before that the Dresden was a rarity, that its red chairs and white leatherette booths and the five-nights-a-week performances from jazz duo Marty & Elayne (who played from 1981 until Marty's passing in 2022) encapsulated a down-to-earth Hollywood glitz woefully fading by the day. Even after a flood tore through the Dresden in 2020, the obligatory rehab stayed true to its decades-old aura – an aura always amplified when sipping a classic cocktail in the lounge. 'The Blood & Sand has been a staple since the 50s, when the originator of the Los Feliz bar Tiki-Ti was bartending here,' says Mark Ferraro, whose late grandfather, Carl, was the Dresden's mastermind. But Ferraro, who oversees the bar, is just as eager to please regulars with originals like the Black Velvet, a blackberry-lavender beauty with gin that most importantly doesn't distract from the past.

HIGH TIDE MARTINI

THE PONTIAC, HONG KONG

Created by **Beckaly Franks**

INGREDIENTS

50 ml (1¾ fl oz) Widges gin

10 ml (⅓ fl oz) Dashi-Infused Vermouth*

2 dashes of Yuzu Tincture**

1 dash of wormwood tincture

Pickled Celery, to garnish***

*For the Dashi-Infused Vermouth

4 g (1 teaspoon) dashi powder (½ standard
   packet)

10 ml (⅓ fl oz) Mancino Secco vermouth

**For the Yuzu Tincture

1 yuzu

60 ml (2 fl oz) high-proof spirit – anything
   100-proof or higher

***For the Pickled Celery

½ celery stick, washed

250 ml (8½ fl oz) white vinegar

250 ml (8½ fl oz) water

1 tablespoon sugar

1 tablespoon salt

3 tablespoons garlic-forward hot sauce
   (the bar uses Crystal)

Every night spent at The Pontiac is bound to be a blissful one because American owner Beckaly Franks has made the wellbeing of her guests a priority. The Pontiac exudes an edgy rock 'n' roll attitude that has helped reinvent the idea of hospitality in Hong Kong, but it's motivating not intimidating. 'We sell acceptance and inclusivity, and that is also translated through our drinks. Our goal is to get you having fun first, then we can make it about the cocktail,' Franks explains. When attention does turn to that drink, however, chances are that what is in the glass will be unexpected, like the High Tide Martini that Franks first developed with her friend Max, who ran the now-closed Hong Kong restaurant Okra. He made the from-scratch wormwood tincture and pickled the celery in a secret hot sauce; she added the dashi-infused vermouth and yuzu, giving rise to a 'sea-forward style of Gibson,' Franks adds. One cocktail in, eyes begin to rest on the room's other amusing sights, like the bulletin board layered with concert flyers, photographs and guest memories, as well as the bar's neon 'Commit to the Lit' sign. The Pontiac's mantra, it's a reminder for one to cultivate their brewing passions. Or, as Franks puts it, 'It's our version of "just do it".'

Recipe method continues overleaf

METHOD

For the Dashi-Infused Vermouth, place the dashi powder into a sealable container. Pour the vermouth over the dashi. Seal the container and let it sit at room temperature for 2 days, then fine strain into a new container via a coffee filter.

For the Yuzu Tincture, mince the yuzu and place into a sealable container. Pour any high-proof spirit, enough to soak the yuzu completely, into the container. Seal the container and let it sit at room temperature for 2–14 days, depending upon strength desired. Then fine strain into a new container via a coffee filter.

For the Pickled Celery, slice the celery stick into spears and place in a Mason jar. Mix the vinegar, water, sugar, salt and hot sauce together. Add to a frying pan and bring to the boil, then pour over the celery. Seal the Mason jar and place in the refrigerator for up to 2 weeks.

Place pickled celery in a chilled cocktail glass and set aside.

Pour the gin, vermouth and both tinctures into a mixing glass with ice and stir. Strain into the chilled cocktail glass, pouring over the pickled celery.

PRELUDE
TO GIN

~~~~~~

A TASTE FOR GENEVER

Amsterdam bartender Tess Posthumus admits she's a bit of a genever geek. 'I love the historic aspect of it. It's the traditional spirit of the Netherlands but it embodies so much in mixology,' she says. Genever, which can only be made in the Netherlands, Belgium, and parts of France and Germany, is often erroneously labelled as Dutch gin, but in fact, it's in a class all its own, one that Posthumus, who is behind the bars Flying Dutchmen Cocktails and Dutch Courage Cocktails, describes as 'the missing link between gin and whiskey'.

Genever blends a malted wine sprung from such grains as rye, corn and barley. It's a neutral spirit infused with juniper and a slew of other botanicals that trace back to 'the Netherlands' monopoly on the spice trade back in the day,' adds Posthumus.

The spirit first made an impression as a medicine in the 1500s and a century later, when British soldiers fought alongside the Dutch against the Spanish in the Eighty Years' War, they fell for genever and brought it back to their homeland. With an assist from William of Orange, who ran the Dutch Republic prior to his years as king of England, Ireland and Scotland, interest in genever grew, until it eventually evolved into gin, England's own version of the spirit. Old Tom Gin, pervasive in the 18th century, was less sweet than genever and richer than the London dry that would later come on the scene and characterise the category.

Early cocktail culture in the Netherlands was basically nonexistent, limited to straight-up drinks and American-style hotel bars that catered to tourists and businessmen, explains Posthumus, yet genever was one of the country's biggest exports to Asia, Australia, Africa and South America, but played an especially vital role in the UK and US, where it had a mighty impact on those bar scenes.

At Flying Dutchmen, Posthumus and her team give their customers a strong cocktail foundation in these centuries-old classics. Barrel-aged Bols genever stars in signatures like the Flying Dutchmen Cocktail, a Gin Fizz spin with lemon juice, speculaas gum syrup, orange bitters and orange flower water, but it's Dutch Courage that puts the spirit at the forefront. Prohibition, World War II and rising demand for London dry gin all helped to obliterate genever exports, but that has changed in recent years, and Dutch Courage is a way 'to re-educate people about genever and show how beautiful the product is,' says Posthumus.

Dutch Courage stocks over 150 genevers across various styles from botanical jonge to malty oude, and customers can educate themselves through tasting flights and such inventive cocktails as the Koko Klapa (coconut oil-washed Hooghoudt raw genever, passionfruit syrup, lime juice and Bittered Sling Kensington bitters) or the savoury Grassy Low Lands (Wynand Fockink Lage Landen Jenever, bay-leaf-sage syrup, grilled pepper liqueur, barley grass and pepper juice, lemon juice, black pepper tincture).

There are certainly similarities between genever and gin, but mixing the former with tonic, for example, is a no-no. Posthumus would much rather drink hers with ginger ale or in a Jack the Ripper.

IT'S A
TRADITIONAL
SPIRIT OF THE
NETHERLANDS,
BUT IT EMBODIES
SO MUCH IN
MIXOLOGY.

JASMINE & LEMONGRASS

PARLOUR, PRAGUE

Created by Jakub Ondříšek

INGREDIENTS

40 ml (1¼ fl oz) citrus-forward gin, such as
   Tanqueray Rangpur, Nikka Coffey or
   Larios
15 ml (½ fl oz) sugar
15 ml (½ fl oz) lime juice
1 small piece of fresh lemongrass, chopped
20 ml (⅔ fl oz) Cold-Brewed Jasmine Tea*
1 barspoon orange marmalade

*For the Cold-Brewed Jasmine Tea
15 g (½ oz) jasmine tea
150 ml (5 fl oz) sparkling water

METHOD

For the Cold-Brewed Jasmine Tea, infuse the
jasmine tea in the sparkling water. Keep the mixture
chilled in the refrigerator for 24 hours before using.

Place the gin, sugar, lime juice and jasmine tea
in a mixing tin with ice. Shake. Strain into a coupe.

Boulevard-like Wenceslas Square, in Prague's New Town, doesn't have the leafy, bohemian charms of Vinohrady nor does it bear the seductive industrial imprint of Holešovice, but it's vital to Prague's history. Close to this must-see meeting place that played a role in such milestones as the Prague Spring and the Velvet Revolution is Parlour. Worrying current events immediately fall away upon entering this cellar bar and hearing the jazz fill the room, seeing the homey assemblage of books, paintings and retro objects. Parlour co-founder Jakub Ondříšek is steadfast in his belief that Parlour is an ephemeral escape, a place to simply make guests happy with delicious cocktails. He shies away from all aspects of razzle-dazzle bar culture, but he does have a predilection for antique crystal glass and recommends serving his Jasmine & Lemongrass in such a vessel. With his Breakfast Martini, London bartender Salvatore Calabrese gave new meaning to the humble jar of marmalade. For this drink, Ondříšek also drifted toward the fruit condiment's bitter notes. 'The Jasmine & Lemongrass is at its best when there is a little space between the surface of the liquid and the rim of the glass. It helps concentrate all flavours,' he says, pointing out that it should summon 'a morning on the porch, right after the rain'.

THE CENTRAL STORY, 1927

LE MAGRITTE BAR & TERRACE AT THE BEAUMONT, LONDON

Created by Antonino Lo Iacono

INGREDIENTS
25 ml (¾ fl oz) Roku gin
15 ml (½ fl oz) Grand Marnier
15 ml (½ fl oz) Campari
15 ml (½ fl oz) Cocchi Vermouth di Torino
10 ml (⅓ fl oz) Muyu Vetiver Gris
mandarin leaf, to garnish

METHOD
Place the gin, Grand Marnier, Campari, Cocchi Vermouth di Torino and Muyu Vetiver Gris in a mixing glass with ice and stir. Strain into a coupette over an ice sphere (the bar makes its own). Garnish with the mandarin leaf.

Just off the glossy Art-Deco-style lobby of The Beaumont, to the left of the amiable doormen standing on the chessboard floor, is Le Magritte Bar & Terrace. The Beaumont, although a relatively new London hotel (it opened in 2014), seems as if it has been stitched into Mayfair's cultural fabric for decades. Le Magritte, with its Fiddleback cherry walls and Martinez-sipping clientele raised on cranberry leather stools, also has the air of a secretive mid-century salon, one that has been dressed in artworks like Slim Aarons photography and café-society paintings by Bernard Boutet de Monvel. Taking pride of place behind the black walnut-stained mahogany bar is the showpiece, Le Maître d'École, Belgian artist René Magritte's painting depicting his contemplative bowler-hatted protagonist bathed in moonlight. Magritte, closely aligned with the Surrealist movement, has imbued such ordinary objects as pipes and green apples with an entrancing sense of disquiet. His contemplative oeuvre has also made an impression on Le Magritte's cocktail menu. While a smoky libation with mezcal and amaro speaks to the artist's meditative *The Empire of Light* series from 1950, 1927's gloomy The Central Story, a rather personal piece that addresses the suicide of Magritte's mother, is represented by this bitter orange-gin number.

CHURCHILL IN A HANDBASKET

VALKYRIE, TULSA

Created by **Aaron Post**

INGREDIENTS
30 ml (1 fl oz) Smoked Tea Gin*
30 ml (1 fl oz) Campari
30 ml (1 fl oz) Carpano Antica vermouth
orange wheel and demerara sugar, to
    garnish

*For the Smoked Tea Gin (makes 1 litre/
    34 fl oz)*
1 litre (34 fl oz) Brokers Gin
3 tablespoons Lapsang souchong tea

METHOD
For the Smoked Tea Gin, combine the gin with the Lapsang souchong tea. Infuse in a jar for 2 hours, shaking regularly. Strain into a new container.

Stir the gin, Campari and Carpano Antica in a rocks glass filled with ice. Liberally sprinkle the orange with sugar and brûlée with mini blowtorch. Garnish the cocktail with the caramelised orange wheel.

At the Greenwood Rising history centre in Tulsa's Greenwood District, visitors learn about the affluent early 20th-century 'Black Wall Street' community that was decimated in the horrifying Tulsa Race Massacre of 1921. Tulsa cannot extinguish that gruesome legacy, but it is on the path to a more just future. Oklahoma's second largest city, it is progressive. Route 66 road trips and the chance to gawk at Art Deco structures like the Pythian Building may reel travellers in, but locals are besotted with the craft breweries, live music performances at The Colony and if it's cocktails they're after, Valkyrie. This Tulsa Arts District bar has a relaxed, industrial-esque vibe with red oak booths and a massive array of booze that has an especially hefty whiskey section. Cocktails at Valkyrie habitually rotate, so one day the Ophelia (aquavit, vermouth amaro, orgeat, lemon, vanilla, lavender tincture) might jump out at the gin buffs; the Churchill in a Handbasket, a smoked Negroni, on another. Aaron Post, Valkyrie's co-owner, was thinking about Cynar, and how the bitter Italian aperitif 'tastes like smoked black tea to me,' he remembers. Wanting to mimic that flavour in a more conventional Campari recipe, he tried a Lapsang souchong tea infusion that 'took to the gin really well,' he adds, 'and I didn't feel like I should over complicate it'. Just like the Valkyrie mindset.

MADE IN NEW ORLEANS

~~~~~~

THE RAMOS GIN FIZZ IS A TIMELESS BEAUTY

A magnificently frothy Ramos Gin Fizz is just as satiating as a milkshake, but beyond its enticing rich and floral profile, the cocktail, like the Sazerac and Absinthe Suissesse, also serves as a portal into New Orleans history. Henry C. Ramos invented the drink in 1888 at the Imperial Cabinet Saloon and it was popularised at his next venture, the Stag Saloon, where a roster of 'Shaker Boys', organised like an assembly line, shook the fizz for 30 seconds each.

Later, the Roosevelt Hotel (now part of the Waldorf Astoria collection) bought the rights to the cocktail, and Huey P. Long, Louisiana governor and US senator, developed a deep love for the Ramos Gin Fizz at the hotel's Sazerac Bar. He even orchestrated a publicity stunt around the cocktail in 1935, hiring The Sazerac Bar's Sam Guarino to fly up to New York and show the unschooled staff at The New Yorker Hotel how to make a respectable Ramos Gin Fizz.

Veteran bartender Nicholas Jarrett, who works at the French Quarter hangout Peychaud's inside the Hotel Maison de Ville, says the Ramos Gin Fizz is 'a one-off, in terms of preparation methodology, texture and flavour. I've lost count of the number of times guests have likened it to 'drinking a cloud'. The story is also great – Ramos gifting the world with its recipe at

the dawn of Prohibition. Long travelling with his own bartenders so he could always have one.'

It's a laborious cocktail indeed, but Jarrett thinks that's also a draw for guests who 'know the drink takes a lot of work to make, and they feel special getting one. It's not that bartenders dislike the labour, it's that taking that long to put together one cocktail invariably detracts from everyone else's experience in the bar by delaying all other cocktail orders.' So, skilled barkeeps have employed time-saving workarounds, including the reliance upon a blender. It's a trick that Jarrett first learned at an event, where a line-up of Vitamixes produced speedy but delicious Ramos Gin Fizzes for the masses. He still uses the appliance at Peychaud's, 'to be able to offer the cocktail expediently' to eager customers. His blender-simple recipe for two is on the next page.

90 ml (3 fl oz) Hayman's Royal Dock Navy
   Strength Old Tom gin
30 ml (1 fl oz) lemon juice
30 ml (1 fl oz) lime juice
60 ml (2 fl oz) simple syrup
42 drops of orange flower water
2 egg whites
90 ml (3 fl oz) double cream
orange twist and reusable straw, to garnish

Combine the gin, lemon juice, lime juice, simple
syrup, orange flower water and egg whites in a bowl
or container. Add the cream to another bowl or
container. In a third bowl or container, combine 120 g
(4 oz) of cobble/Scotsman ice. Prepare two 400-ml
(14-fl oz) Zombie glasses with 30 ml (1 fl oz) club
soda. Pulse the contents of the first bowl in blender;
add the cream and pulse again. Add ice, then blend
on high for 12 seconds. Fill each glass up halfway,
then to just below lip. Let sit for a couple of seconds,
tap the glasses on a bar mat to force the CO_2 up. Top
with club soda until full while rotating for a foam collar.
Garnish with an orange twist and reusable straw.

A MAGNIFICENTLY
FROTHY RAMOS GIN FIZZ IS JUST
AS SATIATING AS A MILKSHAKE,
BUT BEYOND ITS ENTICING
RICH AND FLORAL PROFILE, THE
COCKTAIL, LIKE THE SAZERAC
AND ABSINTHE SUISSESSE,
ALSO SERVES AS A PORTAL INTO
NEW ORLEANS HISTORY.

VILLA VIKTORIA

BECKETTS KOPF, BERLIN

INGREDIENTS

40 ml (1¼ fl oz) gin
15 ml (½ fl oz) red vermouth
10 ml (⅓ fl oz) dry vermouth
15 ml (½ fl oz) Mirabelle eau de vie
7.5 ml (¼ fl oz) orange curaçao

METHOD

Place all the ingredients in a mixing glass with ice.
Stir until well chilled and strain into a cocktail glass.

A photo of the late Irish playwright and novelist Samuel Beckett hangs in the window of Becketts Kopf, a dimly-lit, red-splashed bar in Prenzlauer Berg that elicits a Berlin of yore. Oliver Ebert, who owns Becketts Kopf with his wife Cristina Neves, has a theatre background, but he says Beckett's illuminated visage was happenstance; the idea for it simply coming to his mind 'after we decided to just put a picture in the window instead of a name above it'. Chance is also what prodded Ebert and Neves to open a bar. As Ebert matter-of-factly explains of their motivations, he and Neves wanted to work together 'and I didn't want to wake up early every day'. Basking in morning sleep aside, their instincts were spot-on, for the cocktails at Becketts Kopf, often laced with obscure regional liqueurs, are poetic triumphs. One of the drinks stirred behind the tiled bar is the Villa Viktoria, named for a now-defunct hotel in Düsseldorf built in 1914. Looking to the little-known Claridge Cocktail (purportedly invented at the Hôtel Claridge in Paris by a bartender named Leon Ferrari) for inspiration, the Villa Viktoria fuses gin, vermouth and orange liqueur, but trades the Claridge's apricot brandy for mirabelle plum eau de vie. Holing up with one of these in a cocooning Becketts Kopf armchair confirms that Ebert has succeeded in his ambitions to engender an 'atmosphere of introspection'.

ANGEL SCENT

BLUE BAR AT THE BERKELEY, LONDON

Created by **Raffaele Di Monaco**

INGREDIENTS
35 ml (1¼ fl oz) Bombay Sapphire gin
20 ml (⅔ fl oz) Martini Ambrato vermouth
15 ml (½ fl oz) elderflower cordial
10 ml (⅓ fl oz) verjus
5 ml (1 teaspoon) violet liqueur

METHOD
Place the gin, vermouth, elderflower cordial, verjus and violet liqueur in a mixing glass with ice and stir. Strain into a coupette.

Few cities can compare with London's knockout hotel bars, and of these distinguished haunts, Blue Bar at The Berkeley is indisputably the most aesthetically memorable. The Berkeley originated as a Piccadilly coffee house in the 1700s, then, with some of its original architectural elements in tow, decamped to ritzy Knightsbridge in 1972. When the late designer David Collins crafted Blue Bar in 2000, some of those historic features were entwined in the new space, including decorative carvings by the celebrated early 20th-century architect Sir Edwin Lutyens. Collins then fittingly washed the room in a bespoke shade of soft 'Lutyens Blue', offsetting it with pops of red for an outcome that is at once glam and subdued. The walls, which hover somewhere between sky blue and lavender, are reminiscent of the Aviation's hue. Made with gin, maraschino liqueur, crème de violette and lemon juice, this oft-maligned classic cocktail was first featured in New York bartender Hugo Ensslin's 1916 *Recipes for Mixed Drinks* – in Harry Craddock's *The Savoy Cocktail Book* there is a recipe for a colour-deprived alternative, sans the crème de violette – and has overtly floral tendencies. Blue Bar's Angel Scent is a more proportions-forgiving riff.

TASMANIAN TOUR

≈≈

TASTE OF AUSTRALIA

For years, Australia's beverage culture was synonymous with wine. It's still true, but gin has also been garnering much-deserved attention, propelled by brands like Four Pillars and Brookie's, which illuminate Australia's indigenous herbs and spices. Four Pillars, for example, makes a gin with olive leaf and another infused with Shiraz grapes at its Victoria distillery. Cape Byron Distillery in Byron Bay melds Byron Sunrise finger limes, aniseed and cinnamon myrtle, macadamia, Native River mint and Native raspberry in Brookie's Byron dry gin, and Wild Gin, from Kangaroo Island Spirits, combines boobialla, eau-du-cologne mint, lime zest and pink peppercorn.

The island of Tasmania is particularly rich in gin culture, lined with small, quality distilleries that evoke the landscape in all of their products. Devonport, in the north, is home to Southern Wild Distillery, where Dasher + Fisher gins, including Mountain, Meadow and Ocean varieties, are bolstered with the likes of Tasmanian pepperberry, wakame seaweed, lavender and sloe berries sourced from family-owned producers. Rex Burdon and his son Chris preside over Nonesuch Distillery in Forcett, in southeast Tasmania. They make whisky, but also a sloe gin spawned from sloes grown on old Tasmanian hedgerows. To the west, just north of Hobart, is Lark Distillery, which is well-regarded for its single malt whisky range,

but also for Forty Spotted gins. Forty Spotted Tassie Bush Honey, Forty Spotted Wild Rose and Forty Spotted Citrus & Pepperberry can all be relished at Forty Spotted's contemporary Gin (bar) in Hobart, accompanied by a blending session at the Gin-stitute. Just a few minutes away is the icy, all-white Institut Polaire, where haute tasting menus follow sips of Süd Polaire gins. Along with the invigorating Antarctic dry and overproof expedition strength varieties, there are gins aged in Tasmanian Pinot Noir casks and laced with saffron plucked from Tasmanian crocus fields.

THE SHERRY KICKER MARTINI

GIN PALACE, MELBOURNE

INGREDIENTS

75 ml (2½ fl oz) The Botanist gin
(or any dry gin of preference)
10 ml (⅓ fl oz) Lillet Blanc
5 ml (1 teaspoon) manzanilla sherry
3 drops of orange bitters
lime twist, to garnish

METHOD

Pour the gin, Lillet Blanc, sherry and bitters into
a mixing glass with ice and stir. Strain into a chilled
Martini glass. Garnish with the lime twist.

Exulting in high-quality cocktails on a Saturday night was not the norm in late-1990s Melbourne, but the late visionary Vernon Chalker believed it could be. The city's original gin palace, like many of its rowdy counterparts in 19th-century London, had shut down in a state of disgrace in 1870. More than a century later, Chalker wanted to resuscitate the idea of such an exhilarating venue, forging a new generation of appreciative Martini drinkers in the process. In 1997, he opened his Gin Palace (other establishments would follow), a basement laneway bar dedicated to a spirit that had been pummelled by vodka for decades. Here, in a room appointed in velvet and crystal, he pulled back the curtain on a different universe, one with classic gin cocktails once again at the fore, and people loved what they saw. Drink options are copious at Gin Palace – a Banana Spritz, a mulberry-hibiscus Gin & Tonic – but its Martinis, always served in 'old-school size; 90-ml (3-fl oz) glasses, as Gin Palace's Jess Clayfield describes them, are a smash. Most consequential of these selections is the Martini built to Chalker's preferred specs: 85 ml (3 fl oz) frozen Plymouth gin, 5 ml (1 teaspoon) Noilly Prat vermouth, a lemon twist. Says Clayfield, 'His favourite Martini is always on our menu.'

MISTERIOS

SALMON GURU, MADRID

Created by Diego Cabrera

INGREDIENTS

60 ml (2 fl oz) gin
40 ml (1¼ fl oz) red vermouth
10 ml (⅓ fl oz) Maurin Quina (although
   the bar uses hard-to-find Maurin Quina,
   you can swap in Bénédictine instead)
10 ml (⅓ fl oz) Italicus
10 ml (⅓ fl oz) maraschino liqueur
2 dashes of chocolate bitters
maraschino cherry, to garnish

METHOD

Place the gin, vermouth, Maurin Quina, Italicus, maraschino and bitters in a mixing glass with ice and stir. Strain into a coupette glass and garnish with the maraschino cherry. At the bar, the glass is first smoked with rosemary and presented in dramatic fashion.

Viva Madrid is the bar one goes to when they want to drink a lively Pisco Sour with yellow Chartreuse and smoked honey, when they want to be surrounded by mirrors and colourful wall tiles in a revitalised mid-19th-century taberna in central Las Letras. Salmon Guru, the other Madrid hangout from venerated Argentinean barman Diego Cabrera, is where one goes when they crave a sensorial riot. Aglow in neon lightning bolts and embellished with comic-book BAM! signage and stools seemingly plucked from a vintage Hawaiian motel, the room bursts with Las-Vegas-style energy. Just as madcap and entertaining are the cocktails. A rum libation might be served in an elaborate dragon vessel, one with gin and rhubarb-vanilla syrup extravagantly garnished with a cotton candy wig. Other drinks command attention for their ingredients, like the brandy-forward Samhain with sherry, walnut amaro and homemade pumpkin jam. At first glance, the Chartreuse-hued So Fine, So Fresh resembles nothing more than a sating cooler on a muggy summer day, but an investigation of its flavours – lemon and lime kefir-infused Martin Miller's gin, violet liqueur, coconut water, laurel syrup, matcha tonic – hints at a lurking complexity that underpins all of Salmon Guru's unpredictable moves.

KANJU

THE KEEFER BAR, VANCOUVER

Created by Hugo Finan

INGREDIENTS
45 ml (1½ fl oz) Roku gin
22 ml (¾ fl oz) Shiso-Leaf-Infused
    Chartreuse*
15 ml (½ fl oz) Martini Ambrato vermouth
7ml (¼ fl oz) dry vermouth
Japanese Bitters Company yuzu bitters
lemon twist or shiso leaf, to garnish

*For the Shiso-Leaf-Infused Chartreuse
10 g (½ oz) shiso, chopped
375 ml (12½ fl oz) yellow Chartreuse

METHOD
For the Shiso-Leaf-Infused Chartreuse, add the
shiso to the yellow Chartreuse and let it infuse for
48 hours. Strain out the shiso, and then store in
the refrigerator for up to 6 months. At the bar, the
infusion is sous-vide at 63°C (155°F) for 1 hour.

Place the gin, infused Chartreuse, Martini Ambrato,
dry vermouth and bitters in a mixing glass with ice
and stir. Strain into a chilled coupe. Garnish with a
lemon twist or shiso leaf.

When stirred together in equal parts, gin, sweet
vermouth and green Chartreuse are evocative of the
diamond, ruby and emerald. This trifecta of glittering
gems is what gave the Bijou, a potent sipper included
in the 1900 edition of *Harry Johnson's Bartenders'
Manual*, its name. The Keefer Bar's Kanju, a Japanese-
inspired iteration of the cocktail (in keeping with
the nomenclature, kanju alludes to tide jewels in
Japanese mythology) showcases yuzu- and shiso-leaf-
infused yellow Chartreuse, a reinforcement of the
apothecary-themed Vancouver bar's reverence for
Asian ingredients. Take the Dragonfly, which blends
dragonfruit-infused gin, nigori sake, ginger syrup and
digestive-easing magnolia bark tincture, or the Blood
Moon; its zesty Szechuan and pink peppercorn-
blood orange syrup rejuvenating a backbone of
Hendrick's gin. Located in the city's Chinatown, the
largest in Canada, The Keefer Bar is a love letter to
the neighbourhood's botanical-crammed pharmacies.
These shops, found amid the storefronts tempting
with dim sum and coconut cream buns are where the
bar sources all its herbs, like the immune-boosting
astragalus in the bourbon-Fernet Branca-orgeat
Chinatown Sour. Cocktails aren't medicine, of course,
but The Keefer Bar's elixirs certainly provide an
eye-opening journey into ancient healing practices.

RED PANDA

PANDA & SONS, EDINBURGH

Created by Iain McPherson

INGREDIENTS

1 makrut lime leaf

40 ml (1¼ fl oz) London dry gin

10 ml (⅓ fl oz) lemon juice

100 ml (3½ fl oz) tomato juice

10–20 ml (⅓–⅔ fl oz) sriracha
(depending on preferred spice level)

1–2 dashes of Tabasco sauce

1 cucumber slice

salt and pepper, to taste

25 ml (¾ fl oz) Guinness

sliced cucumber and makrut lime leaf,
to garnish

METHOD

Shred the makrut lime leaf and place in a mixing tin. Add the rest of the ingredients, excluding the Guinness and garnishes. Briefly stir to make sure all the ingredients are mixed together, then proceed to throw the cocktail, by straining it from one tin into another. Strain into a highball glass over cubed ice. Float the Guinness on top. Garnish with a cucumber and makrut lime leaf placed onto a cocktail stick.

The boundary-pushing Iain McPherson, co-owner of the Edinburgh bars Panda & Sons, Hoot The Redeemer and Nauticus, is renowned for his 'switching' technique, wherein the water content of frozen alcohol is replaced with other liquids as a way of concentrating flavours. McPherson's proclivity for science has guided the ethos of Panda & Sons, the bar serving as a platform for a range of lab techniques that span the centrifuge and chamber vacuum to sous vide and ultrasonic infusions. Reached via a barbershop façade, the bar possesses a magnetism that is heightened, say, when the Scotch-based Birdcage, with its flamboyant wisps of cinnamon and clove smoke, touches down on the table, or the bartender explains the process of fractional concentration to the inquisitive patron who ordered the Switched Negroni. As with the Red Panda, sometimes the Panda & Sons effect is more restrained. This Tanqueray Bloody Mary (or Red Snapper to be exact) enhanced with sriracha and Guinness foam defies the perception that this style of cocktail should be relegated to Sunday pancake brunches. As at London's Connaught Bar, where evening requests for the vodka Bloody Mary come as rapidly as those for the tableside trolley Martinis, the Red Panda is a call to recast the Red Snapper as a night-time desire.

MARTINI MAGIC

THE 90S LIVE ON

Some Martinis are just more memorable than others. There's the one at 1930s legend Harry's Bar in Venice, for instance, where everyone else in the room is knocking back Bellinis, but the sight of the bartender donning a white jacket and plopping down an unexpectedly squat tumbler brimming with an extremely dry Martini is a sign that the right decision has been made. For the New York set that frequented Temple Bar in New York's Noho during the halcyon 1990s, the pricey, cartoonishly large Martinis they ordered are likely the ones they can't get out of their heads.

Temple Bar opened in 1989, well before most bar patrons were drinking gin or acquainted with the nuances of vermouth. But two years prior, 'King Cocktail', Dale DeGroff, had ensconced himself behind the bar at Midtown's Rainbow Room, so change was certainly afoot.

Temple Bar was dark – in the absence of social media, it was a choice spot for amorous rendezvous – and the famous cavorted there, swilling garnish-heavy vodka Martinis. This dated glamour wasn't lost on bartender Sam Ross, who fondly remembers going to Temple Bar in 2004 or 2005 with Michael McIlroy, now his partner in the New York and Nashville Attaboy juggernaut.

'It was this decadent haven, we were in our early twenties, and there were massive Martinis with hardly any vermouth that seemed more about quantity than quality that we couldn't afford. But at the time, we remember thinking how beautiful the room felt,' he recalls.

It certainly symbolised a captivating chapter of New York nightlife, but Temple Bar 'got left behind', as Ross puts it, in the rush of mid-aughts cocktail bar openings. People wanted to drink at Pegu Club, PDT and Little Branch.

Ross and McIlroy longed to take over Temple Bar, which shuttered in 2017 after years of decline. They got their wish when they joined forces with Maneesh Goyal and David Rabin and re-opened it in 2021 with subtle design updates and a revamped menu. Now, guests can ogle the original mahogany bar, sink into the same green leather banquettes and drink refined libations like a house Gibson, olive oil-washed vermouth gin Martini and a hard-to-resist bright Blue Negroni that resonate with a more cocktail-savvy crowd.

There is a brand-new clientele these days, but when the old-timers do pop into their favourite haunt from 30 years ago, 'you can see on their faces all the memories coming back,' Ross points out.

THE BARRELED REBELLION

THE GIN ROOM, ST LOUIS

Created by **Natasha Bahrami**

INGREDIENTS

30 ml (1 fl oz) Bluecoat Barrel gin

15 ml (½ fl oz) Dolin Rouge vermouth

15 ml (½ fl oz) light orange liqueur (the bar
   uses New Holland Brewing's Clockwork
   Orange Liqueur from Michigan because
   it's botanical-forward, not sweet)

25 ml (¾ fl oz) Cynar

dehydrated orange wheel, to garnish

METHOD

**Pour the gin, vermouth, orange liqueur and Cynar
into a mixing glass. Stir for 20 seconds and strain
over a large ice cube into a rocks glass. Torch the
dehydrated orange wheel garnish with a mini bar
blowtorch for a few seconds before dropping it
on top.**

Natasha Bahrami was living in Washington, D.C., working in foreign policy research, but it was her side hustles at capital bars that convinced the St Louis native she belonged in the hospitality industry. That 2013 epiphany coincided with the 30th anniversary of her family's Persian restaurant, Café Natasha, and so Bahrami went back to St Louis. Three decades in, Café Natasha yearned for an injection of modernity, and the entrepreneurial Bahrami won her family over with the idea of opening The Gin Room (the multi-city Gin World festival would come later) at the front of the restaurant, a temple to the spirit in all its styles. 'With the food and beverage scene exploding in St Louis I wanted to be part of the force showing how amazing the Midwest actually was,' Bahrami remembers. But St Louis was a beer and bourbon city through and through, 'and though that was a barrier, every single day I worked to dive every guest who would allow me a bit deeper into gin,' she continues. The Barreled Rebellion undoubtedly helped expedite that conversion. An interplay of barrel-aged gin, red vermouth, Cynar and orange liqueur, the cocktail is an efficacious conduit between the whiskey and gin realms.

NAUGHTY TUXEDO

VESPER, BANGKOK

Created by Federico Balzarini

INGREDIENTS

30 ml (1 fl oz) London dry gin
20 ml (²/₃ fl oz) dry vermouth
10 ml (1/₃ fl oz) white crème de cacao
10 ml (1/₃ fl oz) Poire Williams eau de vie
3 dashes of coconut vinegar
cherry, to garnish

METHOD

Add the gin, vermouth, crème de cacao, Poire Williams and coconut vinegar to a mixing glass filled with ice. Stir until well chilled. Strain the drink into a frozen Martini glass. Garnish with the cherry.

Golf and racquetball lure harried New Yorkers some 50 miles north of the city to the idyllic grounds at The Tuxedo Club. This tony clubhouse, dating back to 1886, is where the dashing tuxedo, the dinner jacket and gradual successor to the tailcoat pioneered by the Prince of Wales, regaled American gents for the first time. Then, in 1900, Harry Johnson published a recipe for the Tuxedo in his *Bartenders' Manual*, a close cousin to the Martini with gin, vermouth, maraschino liqueur and orange bitters. Bartenders have been fine-tuning the Tuxedo ever since, formulating their own riffs, like Vesper's Naughty Tuxedo with white crème de cacao and a funky kick of coconut vinegar. Vesper, part of the Foodie Collection's group of restaurants, is in Bangkok's Bang Rak district, where there is no shortage of buzzy venues to imbibe in. But it's Vesper that flaunts the patina of a well-loved European hotel bar, decked out with green marble, teal walls and gold-rimmed mirrors. The bartenders expressing lemon peels over the Earl Grey Gin & Tonics, the orbs of saffron sorbet resting in fragrant pools of Roku gin, yuzu sake, chamomile and sparkling wine in the Beginning | Beginning cocktail – it's all cinematic.

KIKALEIN

LIFE IS BEAUTIFUL, BRUSSELS

Created by Harouna Saou

INGREDIENTS

60 ml (2 fl oz) gin
30 ml (1 fl oz) Pistachio Syrup*
10 ml (1/3 fl oz) dark crème de cacao
30 ml (1 fl oz) lemon juice
30 ml (1 fl oz) egg white or aquafaba
2 dashes of chocolate bitters
crumbled pistachios, to garnish

*For the Pistachio Syrup (makes 1 litre/ 34 fl oz)
200 g (7 oz) pistachios
1 litre (34 fl oz) Simple Syrup (page 9)

METHOD

For the Pistachio Syrup, roast the pistachios in the oven at 180°C (350°F/gas 4) for 5–8 minutes until they start releasing some oils.

Blend the pistachios in a blender or food processor, then add the simple syrup and blend again. Place mixture into container and let it sit overnight. Then strain into a new container via a coffee-filter-lined strainer.

On a trip to New York, Karoline Vlk was struck by a drink served at the former Experimental Cocktail Club that incorporated pistachio. Vlk and her partner, Harouna Saou, had yet to open their Brussels bar Life is Beautiful, but when the time came, Vlk returned to the memory of that liquid dessert, how brightly the pistachio notes shined through. The couple set forth on developing their own rendition, and numerous trials later they were content with the Kikalein, a nutty, chocolatey gin sour that revisits the menu every winter. Vlk and Saou are prolific, conceiving new additions that often have a global bent, like an Okinawa gin highball with seaweed cordial, tomato liqueur and grapefruit kefir. There is a sense of discovery that permeates the bar (and adjacent booze and barware boutique). With friends seated on pillow festooned banquettes snacking on dukkah, the bartenders in the background pouring raspberry eau de vie and frothing chamomile espuma, there is also a rapturous dinner party ambience.

Place the gin, syrup, crème de cacao, lemon juice and egg white in a mixing tin and dry shake. Add ice cubes and shake again. Double strain into a coupe. Garnish with the pistachios.

LAVENDER MERINGUE PIE

QUINARY, HONG KONG

INGREDIENTS

45 ml (1½ fl oz) limoncello
20 ml (⅔ fl oz) Lavender-Infused Gin*
30 ml (1 fl oz) lemon juice
10 ml (⅓ fl oz) egg white
10 ml (⅓ fl oz) Simple Syrup (page 9)
Marshmallow foam**
lavender sugar and dried lemon wheel,
    to garnish

*For the Lavender-Infused Gin
    (makes 750 ml/25 fl oz)*
750 ml (25 fl oz) gin
4 g (1 teaspoon) fresh lavender

**For the Marshmallow Foam*
8 fl oz (¼ fl oz) double cream
20 g (¾ oz) melted marshmallow
3 ml (½ teaspoon) vanilla syrup
    (the bar uses Monin)
6 g (1 teaspoon) egg white

Recipe method continues overleaf

One doesn't get far on the Hong Kong cocktail circuit before hearing the name Antonio Lai. Lai, co-founder of the restaurant and bar collective Tastings Group, is a passionate advocate of 'multisensory mixology', the notion that all five senses can be stimulated by a cocktail. At the flagship bar Quinary, piquing interest on Hollywood Road since 2012, Lai puts that concept into practice with a generous assist from technology. Yes, Quinary is a polished industrial bar, but it is also an R&D laboratory where Lai fiddles with the rotovap, makes lemon-verbena-scented cacao ice cubes for the Gimlet-reminiscent Miss Rosa Fizz, and re-distills spirits like the lemongrass Tanqueray employed in the fizzy elderflower, lime and mint On the Meadow cocktail. The molecular Earl Grey Caviar Martini, a concoction that utilises spherification and flaunts a towering ripple of foam, is a longtime signature, but the bar team is always innovating. In the Haak Lo Mai, for example, Michter's rye is infused with black glutinous rice and draped under a cloud of taro and coconut. It doesn't require a great command of science, but this sweet and sour Lavender Meringue Pie, one of Quinary's bestsellers, is a glimpse into the bar's nerve centre. Let it carry you from dessert to the night's Martini finale.

METHOD

For the Lavender-Infused Gin, pour the gin into a sealable, sterilised bottle and add the fresh lavender. Seal the bottle and let it sit at room temperature for 2–3 days depending upon preferred strength. Line a mesh strainer set over a container with a coffee filter. Strain the gin through the coffee filter into the container.

For the Marshmallow Foam, whisk the cream into the melted marshmallow until the texture turns thick and fluffy. Add in the vanilla syrup and egg white. Whisk well.

Place the limoncello, Lavender-Infused Gin, lemon juice, egg white and simple syrup in a mixing tin and dry shake. Add ice and shake again. Strain into a chilled tall coupe. Top the drink with marshmallow cream. Sprinkle lavender sugar (the bar uses a 1:1 ratio of dried lavender powder and brown sugar) on top of the drink. Slightly torch the surface to create a crème-brûlée-like texture. Garnish with the dried lemon wheel.

LET IT CARRY
YOU FROM DESSERT
TO THE NIGHT'S
MARTINI FINALE.

ABOUT THE AUTHOR

Alia Akkam has long been fascinated by the transporting world of hotels, restaurants and bars, and has a passion for gin that most often manifests in sipping a classic Martini.

Born in New York, in the vibrant, multi-cultural borough of Queens – a place for which she still harbours an intense love – Alia is most drawn to urban settings, wandering aimlessly through crowded streets, gorging on local specialties in small, boisterous restaurants, and observing quirky characters along the way.

Her childhood and adolescent years spent on Long Island, then, were steeped in wanderlust-fuelled daydreams, spinning the retro globe stashed in the upstairs storage room and plucking the Funk & Wagnalls Hammond World Atlas off a shelf in the living room wall unit to pore over images of international flags.

With a penchant for writing short stories as a child, Alia headed to the University of South Carolina's journalism school with dreams of becoming an advertising copywriter and moving to Europe. The former goal morphed into a career writing about restaurants, bars, travel, and design; the latter eventually happened in 2015. After years of working in New York, Alia adventurously moved to Budapest, a city where she knew no one and didn't speak a lick of Hungarian. Now her days of writing are regularly interspersed with Danube strolls and copious amounts of sponge cake consumption in Old World cafes.

Both an architecture and culture geek, Alia is smitten with Art Deco buildings, London's theatre scene, French New Wave films and street art. A devoted nostalgist, she's happiest imbibing in a historic hotel lobby or eating baked ziti in a red leather booth at an old Italian restaurant.

ACKNOWLEDGEMENTS

Simply, this book could not have been written without the enthusiasm and generosity of all the bars that shared their recipes and stories. Thank you to the many bartenders and other industry folks who answered my never-ending questions or sat down to a chat, especially Franck Audoux, Nicholas Bennett, Salvatore Calabrese, Tommaso Cecca, Simon Ford, Núria Girós Navarro, Nicholas Jarrett, Amanjot Johal, Allen Katz, Chris Montana, Tess Posthumus, Garret Richard, Sam Ross and Angus Winchester. I am grateful for their time and insights.

This gin project marks my second collaboration with Hardie Grant UK, and I am once again so pleased to have had the great fortune of working with Eila Purvis, my patient and witty editor. I would also like to tip my hat to designer Maeve Bargman and aptly named illustrator Ella Ginn for capturing the retro spirit of *Behind the Bar: Gin* so imaginatively, as well as Vicky Orchard, whose copyediting prowess elevated this book.

During the writing process, there were a number of people who were particularly kind and helpful I would like to salute, most notably my friend and talented Budapest bartender Dez O'Connell, who pored over and weighed in on every recipe. Sacha Bell, Nola James, Kristy Lysik, Amanda Treece, Caroline Trefler and Amanda Winchester all provided invaluable suggestions, advice and, most importantly, support, while Priyanka Blah, Charlene Rooke, Eleni Nikoloulia and Rebecca Sturt graciously stepped in to assist when they didn't need to.

I would also like to raise a glass to the late, incomparable scribe Jack Robertiello, one of the first people in this wild world of beverage alcohol who encouraged me to find my own place in it. But nothing, of course, would be possible without Aaron Arrowsmith Taylor.

INDEX

40 St Paul's 67

A
absinthe
    Safari Jacket 17
    St Thomas 74
agave syrup: Dunes 70
amaro liqueur: Sunday Gin 18
Amora 49
Angel Scent 148
Angostura bitters
    Baba's Smash 60
    Juliet & Romeo 78
apple cordial: Origins 42
apple juice: Poke Bowl 117–18
Apple-Lauding 64
apple liqueur: Poke Bowl 117–18
apples: Apple-Lauding 64
apricot eau de vie: Gin Blossom
    136
aquafaba: I Am Groot 57
Atlas French 75: 14

B
Baba's Smash 60
The Barreled Rebellion 163
bartenders 8–9
Basil-Chilli Syrup: The First 31–2
basil: The Hope 34
Bees Tease 83
Beet´en Up Negroni 113
beetroot: Beet´en Up Negroni
    113
bitter bianco: Black Velvet 100
Black Velvet 100
blackberry leaf: Amora 49
blackberry syrup: Black Velvet
    100

The Bramble 50–1
Breakfast Martini 121

C
Calabrese, Salvatore 121
Campari
    Beet´en Up Negroni 113
    The Central Story, 1927: 139
    Churchill in a Handbasket
    140
carrot juice: Two Suns 63
celery: High Tide Martini 103–4
The Central Story, 1927: 139
chamomile-infused gin: Snake-Bit
    Sprout 28
Champagne
    Atlas French 75: 14
    Origins 42
Chartreuse
    Baba's Smash 60
    Bees Tease 83
    Grande Gimlet 92–4
    Kanju 157
    Origins 42
cherry liqueur: Beet´en Up
    Negroni 113
chillies: The First 31–2
chocolate bitters
    Clair de Lune 129–30
    Kikalein 167
    Misterios 154
Churchill in a Handbasket 140
cider: Snake-Bit Sprout 28
Clair de Lune 129–30
clarified juice: St Thomas 74
Cocchi Americano: Clair dev
    Lune 129–30
craft distilleries 39–41
cream
    Gin Fizz 143–5
    Lavender Meringue Pie
    168–70

crème de cacao
    Kikalein 167
    Naughty Tuxedo 164
crème de mûre: Amora 49
crème de pêche: Atlas French
    75: 14
crème de rose liqueur: Rose
    Thorn 69
cucumber
    I Am Groot 57
    Juliet & Romeo 78
cucumber juice: St Thomas 74
Cynar
    The Barreled Rebellion 163
    Beet´en Up Negroni 113

D
Darjeeling Limited 132
dashi: High Tide Martini 103–4
The Dewey 77
dill
    A Martini from the North 114
    St Thomas 74
    Two Suns 63
Drama in the LBC 73
Dunes 70

E
Earl Grey tea: Hayman's Tea 54
eau de vie
    Naughty Tuxedo 164
    Villa Viktoria 147
edamame syrup: Poke Bowl
    117–18
egg white
    Gin Fizz 143–5
    Kikalein 167
    Lavender Meringue Pie
    168–70
    My Lady Garden 87–8
    Poke Bowl 117–18
elderflower cordial: Angel Scent
    148

F
Fernet: A Tea In The Desert 25–6
The First 31–2
Ford, Simon 59

G
Genever 107–8
gin
    Amora 49
    Angel Scent 148
    Apple-Lauding 64
    Atlas French 75: 14
    Baba's Smash 60
    The Barreled Rebellion 163
    Bees Tease 83
    Beet´en Up Negroni 113
    Black Velvet 100
    The Central Story, 1927: 139
    Churchill in a Handbasket
    140
    Clair de Lune 129–30
    Darjeeling Limited 132
    The Dewey 77
    Drama in the LBC 73
    Dunes 70
    The First 31–2
    Gin Blossom 136
    Gin Fizz 143–5
    Grande Gimlet 92–4
    Hayman's Tea 54
    High Tide Martini 103–4
    The Hope 34
    I Am Groot 57
    Jasmine & Lemongrass 110
    Juliet & Romeo 78
    Kanju 157
    Kikalein 167
    Larkin G&T 37
    Lavender Meringue Pie
    168–70
    Little Prince 122–5

A Martini from the North 114
Misterios 154
Mother of Water 46
My Lady Garden 87–8
Nashi & Matcha 97–8
Naughty Tuxedo 164
Origins 42
Poke Bowl 117–18
Poppy Collins 45
Red Panda 158
Rose Thorn 69
Safari Jacket 17
The Sherry Kicker Martini
153
Shinko Sour 84
Snake-Bit Sprout 28
St Thomas 74
Sunday Gin 18
A Tea In The Desert 25–6
Two Suns 63
Villa Viktoria 147
Gin & Tonic 20–3
Gin Blossom 136
Gin Fizz 143–5
Grand Marnier: The Central
Story, 1927: 139
Grande Gimlet 92–4
grapefruit: Grande Gimlet 92–4
grapefruit juice: The Dewey 77
grapes: Amora 49
green tea: Little Prince 122–5
grenadine: Rose Thorn 69
Guinness: Red Panda 158

H
Hayman's Tea 54
Herb-Infused Kombucha: The
First 31–2
herbs 127
High Tide Martini 103–4
history of gin 21–2, 39–41, 59,
107–8

honey
    Apple-Lauding 64
    Larkin G&T 37
    Shinko Sour 84
honey syrup
    Bees Tease 83
    The Dewey 77
    Hayman's Tea 54
    My Lady Garden 87–8
    Two Suns 63
The Hope 34

I
I Am Groot 57
Italicus: Misterios 154

J
Jasmine & Lemongrass 110
Johal, Amanjot 67
Juliet & Romeo 78

K
Kanju 157
Kikalein 167
Kombucha: The First 31–2

L
lactic vanilla cordial: Clair de
    Lune 129–30
Lapsang souchong tea: Churchill
    in a Handbasket 140
Larkin G&T 37
The Last Word 127
Lavender Meringue Pie 168–70
lavender water: Black Velvet 100
lemon juice
    Apple-Lauding 64
    Atlas French 75: 14
    Baba's Smash 60
    Bees Tease 83
    Darjeeling Limited 132
    The Dewey 77

Drama in the LBC 73
Dunes 70
The First 31–2
Gin Fizz 143–5
Hayman's Tea 54
Kikalein 167
My Lady Garden 87–8
Poppy Collins 45
Red Panda 158
Rose Thorn 69
Safari Jacket 17
wo Suns 63
lemon twist
    The First 31–2
    Hayman's Tea 54
lemon wheel
    The Dewey 77
    Poppy Collins 45
lemongrass: Jasmine &
    Lemongrass 110
lemongrass juice: St Thomas 74
Lillet Blanc
    Safari Jacket 17
    The Sherry Kicker Martini
    153
lime juice
    Gin Fizz 143–5
    I Am Groot 57
    Jasmine & Lemongrass 110
    Juliet & Romeo 78
    Larkin G&T 37
    Poke Bowl 117–18
    Snake-Bit Sprout 28
    A Tea In The Desert 25–6
lime zest: Mother of Water 46
limes: Grande Gimlet 92–4
limoncello: Lavender Meringue
    Pie 168–70
Little Prince 122–5

M
mace tincture: Larkin G&T 37

maraschino liqueur
    Drama in the LBC 73
    Misterios 154
    Safari Jacket 17
marmalade: Jasmine &
    Lemongrass 110
marshmallows: Lavender
    Meringue Pie 168–70
A Martini from the North 114
Martinis 161
mastiha: Baba's Smash 60
matcha tea: Nashi & Matcha
    97–8
Maurin Quina: Misterios 154
mint
    I Am Groot 57
    Juliet & Romeo 78
    Rose Thorn 69
    A Tea In The Desert 25–6
Misterios 154
Mother of Water 46
My Lady Garden 87–8

N
Nashi & Matcha 97–8
Naughty Tuxedo 164
Negroni 20–3

O
olive brine: The Hope 34
olives
    The Hope 34
    Sunday Gin 18
orange bitters
    The Dewey 77
    Gin Blossom 136
    The Sherry Kicker Martini
    153

orange curaçao
    A Tea In The Desert 25–6
    illa Viktoria 147
orange flower water: Gin Fizz
143–5
orange juice: Two Suns 63
orange liqueur: The Barreled
Rebellion 163
orange slice
    Baba's Smash 60
    Gin Blossom 136
Origins 42

P

pear juice: Nashi & Matcha 97–8
pepper: Poppy Collins 45
Peychaud's bitters: Dunes 70
pineapple juice
    Drama in the LBC 73
    I Am Groot 57
    Snake-Bit Sprout 28
    St Thomas 74
pineapple: Larkin G&T 37
pistachios: Kikalein 167
Plymouth Gin Distillery 59
Poke Bowl 117–18
Poppy Collins 45
port: Amora 49
Posthumus, Tess 107–8
Prohibition 7–8, 107
prosecco: Sunday Gin 18

R

raspberry liqueur: My Lady
    Garden 87–8
Red Panda 158
rhubarb liqueur: Poppy Collins
45
Richard, Garret 81
Rose Thorn 69
rose water: Juliet & Romeo 78

rosemary
    Apple-Lauding 64
    Bees Tease 83
    Dunes 70

S

Safari Jacket 17
saline solution: Atlas French
75: 14
The Saturn 81
seltzer: Poppy Collins 45
The Shanty 40–1
sherry
    Dunes 70
    The First 31–2
    Grande Gimlet 92–4
    The Sherry Kicker Martini
    153
    Sunday Gin 18
    Shinko Sour 84
shiso: Kanju 157
simple syrup
    Atlas French 75: 14
    Baba's Smash 60
    Darjeeling Limited 132
    Drama in the LBC 73
    Gin Fizz 143–5
    I Am Groot 57
    Juliet & Romeo 78
    Mother of Water 46
    Snake-Bit Sprout 28
    St Thomas 74
    A Tea In The Desert 25–6
Snake-Bit Sprout 28
soda water
    Amora 49
    Mother of Water 46
    Sunday Gin 18
sour mix: Amora 49
spearmint leaves: Baba's Smash
60

sriracha: Red Panda 158
St-Germain liqueur: Hayman's
    Tea 54
St Thomas 74
strawberry syrup: Poppy Collins
45
sugar syrup: Amora 49
Sunday Gin 18

T

Tasmania 151
tea
    Churchill in a Handbasket
    140
    Darjeeling Limited 132
    The First 31–2
    Hayman's Tea 54
    Jasmine & Lemongrass 110
    Little Prince 122–5
    Nashi & Matcha 97–8
    A Tea In The Desert 25–6
Temple Bar 161
thyme
    Mother of Water 46
    Shinko Sour 84
tomato juice: Red Panda 158
tonic water
    The Hope 34
    Larkin G&T 37
    Nashi & Matcha 97–8
    Safari Jacket 17
turmeric
    Darjeeling Limited 132
    Two Suns 63
Two Suns 63

U

umeshu: Poke Bowl 117–18

V

Vecchio Amaro del Capo:
Sunday Gin 18

verjus
    Angel Scent 148
    Shinko Sour 84
vermouth
    Angel Scent 148
    Apple-Lauding 64
    The Barreled Rebellion 163
    The Central Story, 1927: 139
    Churchill in a Handbasket
    140
    Gin Blossom 136
    High Tide Martini 103–4
    Kanju 157
    A Martini from the North 114
    Misterios 154
    Naughty Tuxedo 164
    Sunday Gin 18
    Villa Viktoria 147
Vetiver Gris: The Central Story,
    1927: 139
Villa Viktoria 147
vinegar: Larkin G&T 37
violet liqueur: Angel Scent 148
vodka: Grande Gimlet 92–4

W

watermelon juice: Dunes 70
wine, white: Mother of Water 46

Y

yuzu bitters: Kanju 157
yuzu: High Tide Martini 103–4